anxiety
CALMING THE CHAOS WITHIN

SHARED EXPERIENCES AND PRACTICAL
STRATEGIES TO CREATE POSITIVE CHANGE.

GAIL A. BARRETT, MA, RCC

 FriesenPress

Suite 300 - 990 Fort St
Victoria, BC, V8V 3K2
Canada

www.friesenpress.com

ISBN
978-1-9995250-1-9 (Hardcover)
978-1-9995250-0-2 (Paperback)
978-1-9995250-2-6 (eBook)

1. PSYCHOLOGY, EMOTIONS

Distributed to the trade by The Ingram Book Company

In appreciation for Anxiety: Calming the Chaos Within

With lessons gleaned from her own experience (which is a great deal in itself, and a fascinating part of the book) Gail offers a warm, unconventional, well-researched, easily accessible, upbeat manual to manage anxiety. This book is chock full of strategies, set with easy to follow guidelines and a wonderful sense of humourous play that carries the book along, saying "You can do it!"

Carrie Bahm MA, RCC

***

I highly recommend that you keep this must-read reference book by your side. It provides practical, easy to follow processes that allow you to look at your anxiety and learn how to deal with it. I will be purchasing the book for my family and friends.

Norma Green
Former Director, Men's Spiritual Healing Lodge

***

I am a proponent of CBT or other types of therapies in combination with or as a substitution for medications when applicable. When you have an entire shed of tools to make your project easier, why not utilize everything at your disposal? This book contains a lot of tools!

Dr. Michele McCue, BCPP

***

Gail Barrett's achievement is evident when she compassionately completes this commitment to share her personal experiences and knowledge as a clinical counsellor/therapist. The personal sharing, lessons learned, knowledge of experts and strategies/tasks to manage anxiety chaos are abundant and practical.

Glenda Hanson, MSW

***

An experiential approach to the human struggle with anxiety and how it manifests in daily living. Gail has addressed the realities of coping with anxiety, while encouraging us to befriend it in order to successfully respond to it. A practical and empowering guide to one of life's most common challenges.

Aleitha Ward MPS (AT), RSW

***

I accessed useful information about the origins of anxiety and how and why it manifests. I learned that I have a choice as to whether or not I allow it to run my life. Gail provides tools to kick anxiety to the curb. The tools are practical, easy to incorporate into a daily practice of self-care, and sometimes, down-right fun. Gail writes from the perspective of a clinical therapist, and human being who has experienced anxiety since childhood. Her book comforted me when I was experiencing high levels of anxious behaviours. I am at last on the path of self-rediscovery and living a life without anxiety.

Judy Walker
Post-Anxiety Bloomer

Table of Contents

For
My grandson Leon Elliot Nadin Barrett
My granddaughter Madeline Harper Nadin Barrett
You fill me up with joy and love.

Go boldly forth!

and
Their magnificent parents,
Jennifer Barrett and Russell Nadin
You know how to do it right.

PART ONE

What Is Anxiety, and Am I Stuck With It?

CHAPTER ONE
Stuck in the Muck

Anxiety is an ancient and important survival mechanism that keeps us from wandering into danger. I know from experience, however, that when anxiety runs amuck, it can be paralyzing. It can stop us cold, and it can affect us physically, mentally, emotionally, and spiritually. It can assume control of our lives.

Perhaps you're familiar with the experience of anxiety. You may have encountered it in the past, or perhaps you're feeling it at this very moment to a mild, moderate, or even severe degree. If it's not *your* experience, it may be happening to someone you love. If that's the case, you'll want to understand exactly how it affects them and how you might help them. I know from my own experience, and from others who have shared their stories with me, that anxiety can be crippling in terms of how we feel and behave. It can, to a small or large extent, narrow the scope of our daily lives. Most of us, when we encounter over-the-top anxiety for the first time, are left wondering, "What in the hell is happening to me?"

Michelle Magafas Flood lives with anxiety on an almost daily basis, and it leaves her feeling utterly exhausted. Here is how she described her reality:

"First my mind races, and I can't breathe. Then my arms and legs feel like they are worthless to me. My heart races, and I'm afraid to even give audible words to the terror that I can't escape. When things go well, in my head there has to be some underlying bad thing at work. If I'm fine, then my kid is in danger. There are no words that come to mind that could console me, because there are no guarantees for anyone's safety. Which brings on the feelings of hopelessness and makes me feel like why even bother getting out of bed? Now imagine that as a loop, playing in your head most days, over and over. That's my anxiety."

Michelle is not alone. Millions of people suffer because of anxiety, often in silence. Because I am so aware of this suffering, I have become passionate about sharing what I have learned about anxiety and what can be done about it. As a clinical therapist, I deal with issues of grief, depression, self-esteem, stress, addictions, relationships, abuse of all kinds, and many other matters. I also encounter anxiety in a large percentage of my clients, men and women alike, adults and children. I see it in my family, my friends, and in complete strangers. It is widespread, and we as a society are often floundering in the dark, seemingly unable to help one another.

This book is not a scholarly undertaking, but rather a sharing of my personal connection to this phenomenon and the knowledge that I have accumulated that will empower you to make a difference in your own encounter with anxiety. I will focus on this experience and the potential to use specific strategies that *will work* to combat your anxiety. I will not focus on the academic, theoretical, or boring but will point out research if I think it will be of interest to you. The book will be wildly motivating, and entertaining, and hopefully very helpful to boot. (As you can see, I'm setting us both up for success here.)

I won't be citing medical journals. When I have discovered authors that I like, I'll introduce you to their work by sharing why I liked them and how they have impacted my thinking. I'll most likely encourage you to read their books. If I have connected with some random person who has given me a great idea, I'll tell you about that idea.

Much of what I have to tell you will come from my own personal story and the experience of others I am connected to.

I'm not going to tell you how to read this book. As you will come to understand, I believe that you are the best expert about you and your needs, and that you are fully capable of deciding how you want to tackle the book. If you start at the beginning, you'll discover a foundation that will keep you solid as you begin to make changes in your life. But if you are overwhelmed with panic attacks, you may choose to start with that chapter and then backtrack to the beginning. Whatever you decide will be just fine. This book is yours to determine the best solutions for you, in whatever way works for you.

I'll digress for a moment to discuss how we use words and why they matter. There is currently some thinking that the phrase *panic attack* should not be used because it might create the impression that what you are experiencing is worse than it actually is. I know that the word *panic* creates changes in my body – faster heart rate, tightening of muscles. The idea of being attacked doesn't make me happy either. Despite this, I've chosen to use that phrase in this book because I think that most people (especially those who have experienced it) will know exactly what I'm talking about when I use the words *panic attack*; however, you may wish to remove the phrase from your vocabulary moving forward. Perhaps you will want to create your own less threatening description of what is happening to you in order to minimize its power. I think if I had panic attacks, I would probably name them *Hellish Hiccups.* Here's the thing – I can invite the big, ugly *Hellish Hiccups* over to visit me or not. If she comes to my door uninvited, I can tell her to leave. I know how to stand up to that bully. And you will learn how to do that too.

It will not be necessary for our purposes here to addle your brain with the more complicated medical mechanisms of anxiety which, by the way, are not entirely understood even by the experts. I will touch on them, and if you are interested, I would encourage you to learn more.

There is one more thing to add about how this book is written. I might occasionally make light of the experience of anxiety, and your anxious thinking and behavior, to encourage you to laugh at yourself. When I do this, please know that I am not laughing *at* you. Learning to relax your sensitivity (which can be a self-protective behavior) is an important first step in managing your anxiety. I know this from experience. Laughter *will* help to disempower this *thing* that has its grip on you.

What you need right now is a way to determine the origin of your own anxiety, the fuel that keeps it going, and some strategies that will work to help you decrease and hopefully eliminate it. I have lots of those to share with you. I don't consider myself to be a medical expert by any stretch, but I do know a lot that might be helpful to you.

What Makes Me an Authority, of Sorts?

Who am I, and why do I feel I have something important to say about anxiety? I'm a 68-year-old mother, grandmother, Registered Clinical Therapist, and spiritual optimist. I am working to be as physically fit and as healthy as I can be. A couple of years ago, I added a purple streak to my hair for a few months and have recently recreated the same look at the request of my three-year-old grand-daughter. The streak is a reminder to me about how I want to live the remainder of my precious days – a reminder that I always want to make the bold choice.

What is that bold choice for me? I want to live every moment, sharing the wisdom I have gleaned through some hard knocks and some really positive experiences. I now stand up to be counted, letting go of the fear of someone else's response to my thoughts, words, and actions. I speak out about the things I care about – the importance of being inclusive and compassionate, the urgency of taking care of our earth, the power of kindness, and the joy that comes with knowing that I am making a difference. I am using my voice. My grandchildren and their parents are the future, and they are very precious to me. I want to know that I play a small yet positive part in how their lives will unfold.

The getting physically fit part is my biggest challenge because I love chocolate and I don't love exercise (although I'm learning to). I am learning that when I eat lots of vegetables, I actually begin to crave them. I'm feeling more empowered every time I step foot in the gym (and, you know, do some exercise). I have learned much about self-care and also about having balance in my life, and I strive to do a good job in both areas, knowing that if I don't, I will certainly begin to feel anxious. Yes, I have experienced anxiety in my life, and I have learned many strategies to monitor and control that anxiety. Now, most of the time, I no longer feel unwarranted anxiety, but when it begins to creep up on me, I recognize it more quickly and employ strategies to take care of it.

Through my work as a therapist, it's become apparent to me that anxiety and depression are becoming more prevalent in North America and perhaps all over the world. Although I have clients with a myriad of issues, anxiety is by far the most prevalent. Doctors are throwing pills at us and are sometimes offering precious little else. We have named so many mental health conditions, and the pharmaceutical companies have come up with a pill for all of them. Pills alone are not solving the problem.

Anxiety and depression are often like the dog chasing its tail. It's sometimes hard to determine where one begins and the other ends. One can create the other, and it really doesn't matter which comes first. When your life is riddled with anxiety, and you are stuck, you can certainly become depressed. If your depression doesn't lift, you may become very anxious about it.

Sometimes one of the first things we do when feeling anxious or depressed is to go to our family doctor. GOOD FIRST STEP. Sadly, some doctors are ill equipped and seriously undereducated about anxiety. The Western medical model, when it comes to mental health, is often about medicating to make the problem (symptoms) go away. All too often what we are really doing is simply *masking* the symptoms, while the problem remains. If your doctor doesn't understand anxiety, I urge you to find one who does. Ask your friends, look online, do whatever you need to do. You can even ask your doctor for a referral to someone who works with anxiety.

In this book you'll learn, in part from the stories I share, the ways in which you might begin to change your thinking and behaviour right at the outset. I would like to suggest that you get a journal and record the strategies you would like to try, and also the strategies that you actually *do* try, and then highlight the strategies that make a difference for you. If you're not opposed to making your own presence known in this a book, I encourage you to live in your copy, and by that, I mean get out your ruler (if you need a really straight line), your pencil, your highlighter, your sticky notes – and let this book be your place to create what works for you. Underline, write in the margins, draw pictures. It's really okay to do that! Let this book be your reminder, your go-to reference, and your cheering squad. Talk back to me if you want to.

Remember, the strategies you choose to employ will take practice. Don't give up on something if it doesn't work immediately. You will learn a new way to think about anxiety, because anxiety is very much a *thinking thing.* Yes, I meant to use the word thing. More on that later.

I believe that you'll relate to what I have to say because I find many universal aspects to our shared anxiety experience – my own, my family's, my friends', and my clients'. It is in the sharing of these challenges that we also find the opportunity to share our solutions.

I sometimes think that we have medicalized far too many things. When I was a kid, I was not told that I had an anxiety disorder. For me, that would have felt like a life sentence, accompanied by feelings of helplessness and powerlessness. Fortunately, I was considered to be *a worry wart*. Which label do you think might hold the most power over me? It seems to me that the minute we come up with a medical name for something and a drug to go with it, the situation somehow becomes more ominous. I'm not discounting the relief of finally finding a diagnosis and treatment for a health problem. I am, however, talking to a certain extent about catastrophizing a behaviour that can be unlearned. I realize that I am going out on limb here, but I would really like us all to consider anxiety not only as medical condition, but also as a behaviour that can be altered.

My Thoughts About Medication

I'm not opposed to medication. Pills do sometimes have a place in our treatment of anxiety and depression. Medication may be the mechanism that eases anxiety or lowers it enough for people to actually begin to practice the strategies that have thus far eluded them. A Doctor of Pharmacology recently explained to me that medicating for anxiety is a tricky business because the brain is very complicated, and medications must respond to this complexity. She said that it is sometimes difficult to "get the right mix" to actually make the medications effective. This would suggest that if you do decide that anxiety medication is something you want to employ, don't be afraid to try more than one type of medication if the first type does not work for you.

Although medication is effective for some, it's been my experience that pills without creative, solid strategies and real action are
not likely to decrease your anxiety significantly or long-term. Pills
sometimes have side effects, and sometimes we take pills to take
care of the side effects from those other pills. Do you see where
this is going?

Doctors now, much more so than ten or twenty years ago, are more likely to refer their clients to counsellors, therapists, social workers, psychologists, and/or psychiatrists. GOOD SECOND STEP. If they don't offer to make that referral for you, tell them you want a referral. Advocate for yourself.

WARNING!

Does that word make you feel anxious? It is supposed to – it's okay. Your anxiety keeps you from wandering into dangerous territory. The warning I wish to give you is this: **please do not stop taking any medication without doctor supervision.** That would not be safe. First, learn a few strategies, then chat with your doctor, and make a plan that works for you. It may be that a combination of medication and a variety of other strategies will be the most effective for you.

You will be the best person to determine what your approach will be. You and I are similar in that regard. I am an authority in my own life. I have learned from my own experience, the experience of others, many teachers, and many books, just as you have. Your experience is valid. Only you can make a decision that makes a difference for you. If there is anything I have learned in the past 68 years, it is this: if you take one step, just one step, something will change.

I know that there are many *causes* of anxiety, but I also know that there are many *solutions*. We're going to be using visualization as one of the important tools to help you manage your 'muck,' so let's try and visualize how anxiety is much like being stuck in the mud. Before we start, I want to spend a moment thinking about the power of visualization. Norman Doidge, M.D., is a researcher, psychiatrist, and psychoanalyst, and he has written a wonderful book for brain non-experts (like me) to help us all understand our brains a little better. He, among others, has influenced my thinking in terms of helping me understand the power of visualization. You may wish to check out his book, *The Brain that Changes Itself.*

Basically, what I have learned is that when our brain *imagines* something, it's virtually the same as *doing* that thing, and that when we imagine something, it actually changes the physiology of our brain synapses. Sports psychologists use this practice with their athletes all the time. This could be a very powerful force for the positive in our lives, but by the same token, if we continuously imagine negative scenarios, it can also be a very negative force in our lives. One of the many positive aspects of using our imagination is that it also works very well with children.

Let's try to visualize now how anxiety is very much like being stuck in the mud. We'll use my own childhood experience as an example.

There was a huge field out behind our home, and in the springtime, it was filled with crocuses, bluebells, and dandelions. I loved to play there. One spring, when I was about 6 years old, my friend Lorna and I donned our rubber boots and ventured out into the field to explore. We both had a crush on the nice teenage neighbour boy, and it was our plan to make mud cakes and put them on his doorstep. I guess we thought our mud cakes would really impress him. It didn't take too long for both of us to become hopelessly stuck in the mud.

Lorna and I pulled and yanked on our rubber boots to no avail. We were stuck but good. There was only one thing to do — call for help. It seemed to take forever, but it was probably only a minute or two before our mothers arrived. They assessed the situation and came up with a plan. By this time, Lorna and I were frightened and in tears. It was not fun to be held hostage by the mud.

It was much too muddy for our mothers to come in the field themselves. Off they went to get some nice long boards. Very gingerly, our moms placed the boards one in front of the other and slowly made their way to us, walking on the path that they had created with the boards.

Once my mother reached me, she carefully lifted me from my boots and placed me on the board. She then yanked on my rubber boots, and with a sucking, squelchy noise, my boots slurped up out of the mud. I still vividly recall the sound of the boots breaking free. Ever so slowly and carefully, we made our way back to dry land. The tears stopped and the anxiety eased.

Being stuck in the mud leaves you without the ability to move. The way back to dry land, to *normal,* looks impossible. It is important to understand how you got there to avoid repeating the mistake, but at that moment you really just want to get out of there. But you have no tools to make it happen. Doesn't that sound a little bit like anxiety?

Creating the Path to Safety

What were the important ingredients that allowed for a successful outcome to our little escapade? First, Lorna and I were both adventuresome and not afraid to try new things. This is very important when it comes to getting a handle on your anxiety: having the courage to try something new. If you are going to try something new, it will be absolutely necessary for you to place yourself in a position of *beginner*, a place where you're vulnerable because you're doing something new, and you don't know exactly how to do it. You will need to be ready to try, possibly fail, try again, not do it perfectly, and try again. That takes courage, but the rewards are built into the process, and that's the carrot that will keep you moving forward.

The second ingredient that allowed our successful outcome is that we weren't afraid to ask for help when we didn't know what to do. Often when we experience anxiety, we suspect that no one will truly understand, or perhaps we worry that people will think that we're flawed or weak. We may feel embarrassed or vulnerable, and as a result we keep our troubles to ourselves. Or we may think that since we've tried pills, or tried one or two strategies, and they didn't work, why bother trying something else? But if you're like Lorna and I – so stuck that there is no way to handle it without help – then you are ready for the next step: asking for help and believing that help is out there for you.

The third step is easy, for some: accepting the help that is offered. As I said, for some this will be easy, but for others, accepting help may be difficult, perhaps because of misplaced pride or a feeling that you are not worthy. But knowing that you need help and accepting help when offered is a very important step in this process.

Once you decide to accept help, it is important to be discerning about the help you are offered, and that is your fourth step. If my mother had decided that I should run back to her, through the mud, while she hollered encouragement my way, well, you can see where that would have taken me – stuck, in the same spot, or perhaps a new spot...but still stuck.

It's the same with anxiety. If my doctor says, "Here, have a bottle of Ativan for when you're really in panic mode," I hope that I would be discerning enough to know that this might treat my symptoms, momentarily, but not really deal with the root of the problem. A short-term fix is not a long-term fix, pure and simple. Being brave enough to try something new, asking for help, accepting help, and discerning what is truly helpful *for you* are all important ingredients for success.

We have our foundation. Now we will build on it.

CHAPTER TWO
Attitude is Everything

As you set out on this journey to discover the reality of your own anxiety and how you can best cope with it, I want to tell you that attitude really is everything. If you believe you can't ever beat this beast, you never will. If you believe in the power of your brain to create anxiety, and if you believe in the power of that same brain to tame anxiety, then you are very likely going to tame it. Believing every day that you have a choice as to how you will live that day is step number one. You get to choose.

We have all known people who are negative about everything, and we've known people who are generally positive – the old glass half-full, glass half-empty scenario. I'll be talking a lot about focusing on the positive, but I don't want to discount the negative altogether.

Gabor Maté, M.D., is a hero to me, of sorts. I don't mean the kind with a cape, who rushes in to save the day. He is not that sort. Rather, he is a truly mortal man who uses his considerable intelligence and talent to work, in part, with people who have addictions, trauma, and other life challenges in Vancouver. His thinking about including the negative in our reality has influenced the way I think about living with a positive attitude while also acknowledging the negative in our lives. I love the way his brain works. He's written three books, and you may wish to have a look at his book about stress, *When the Body Says No.*

The reality is, we are not doing ourselves any favours when we refuse to recognize the negative in our lives. When we do acknowledge the negative, we can begin to take control of the situation by formulating a plan to make things better. If we don't have control over the situation, we can begin to grieve, if that is appropriate, or to let go, if that is appropriate. I once knew a man who, when asked how things were going, always responded, "Couldn't be better!" even when the situation was less than positive. He was the master of failing to confront his own reality, and it caused him no end of difficulty.

The really important point here is that we must be able to trust that we can handle what comes our way, good or bad, because if we can't trust that we can handle what comes our way, we will likely feel very anxious. We will talk more about trusting yourself, your own feelings, and your own decisions, because self-trust is key to managing anxiety.

Sometimes our anxiety stems from something which we do not control, and sometimes it stems from things that we do control. We will discuss what we need to do in both cases to promote more confidence and less anxiety. I've also found that balance plays a key role in the level of my own anxiety. Often in my life, when things are not going well, it is a question of balance, which is why I will be talking about the importance of self-care later in this book. I've learned some hard lessons on that issue. You may wish to consider the mental, physical, emotional, and spiritual balance in your own life when anxiety rears its head.

I came across a quote some years ago that said everything to me about attitude. I don't recall where I found it. It did say that the author was unknown, and I made a note of that, because I like to give credit where credit is due. Everything I have learned about anxiety, everything I am putting in this book, has come from my own experience or someone else's experience or knowledge. Maybe I read it. Maybe a client shared with me, or maybe a teacher taught me. I want to take this moment to thank them all for filling me up with information that I hope will be helpful to you.

Now, back to attitude and the quote that has stuck with me over the years. Here it is:

"The longer I live, the more I realize the impact of attitude on life. Attitude, to me, is more important than facts.

It is more important than the past, than education, than money, than circumstances, than failures, than successes, than what other people think or say or do. It is more important than appearance, giftedness, or skill. It will make or break a company… an organization… a home.

The remarkable thing is, we have a choice every day regarding the attitude we will embrace for that day. We cannot change our past… we cannot change the fact that people will act in a certain way. We cannot change the inevitable. The only thing we can do is play on the one string we have, and that is to choose our attitude. And in choosing our attitude, we will choose our experience for that day.

I am convinced that life is 10% what happens to me and 90% how I react to what happens to me. And so it is with you. We are in charge of our own attitudes. We are in charge of our own experience." Author Unknown

My attitude is informed by the things I do and learn every day, and occasionally I learn from reading fiction. Storytelling is a powerful tool that helps us to understand how to navigate the challenges we all face. I recently read a book called *The Clay Girl* by Heather Tucker. It is the story of sisters who have come from miserable, abusive circumstances and how they survive and, in some cases, thrive despite their early beginnings. I love the book because it speaks to this question of attitude.

I see the same thing over and over again in my clients. They may come from similar situations, but some of them choose to learn how to successfully survive and thrive, while others find it much more challenging. What is this thing called resilience, and why are some more resilient than others? I don't have the answer to that, but I suspect that attitude plays an important part. Your attitude, and having even one person who believes in you, one person who has your back, will make all the difference. Therein lies the challenge, because we often learn our attitude from the environment in which we are raised.

I have encountered some clients who approach their lives with the attitude that they will be as much unlike their parents as they possibly can be, because they're aware of the negative things they've learned from their parents' behaviours and attitudes. I am encouraged to know that just as behaviour can be learned, it can also be unlearned, and then we can learn *new* behaviour. We have about 100 billion brain cells called neurons. Every time we listen, talk, or practice something, new fibers called dendrites grow out of our neurons. Our learning is built as our network of dendrites grows higher and higher with new dendrites sprouting from existing ones. New connections can form and the internal structure of existing synapses can change. Our brain actually engages in synaptic pruning during such changes, deleting the neural connections that are no longer necessary or useful, and then strengthening the connections that are necessary or useful. This is why I know that you can change your relationship with anxiety. Your brain will help you to do it.

All of this is very empowering, especially when you realize that you can begin to empower your own children at a young age. You can give them the skills they will need to make good choices and you can affirm them when they do so, while gently guiding them when they do not. You can begin to build self-confidence in your children at a young age, to help them learn to trust themselves. You can teach them about what they control, and what they do not control, and about how their attitude will impact every part of their lives. Most importantly, you can positively mentor them by your words and actions, every single day, in terms of how they learn to deal with anxiety.

I was recently gifted with a wonderful book called *My Mind Book* by Fiona Williams. I think it is a brilliant guide to help children use their very own brains to self-regulate their emotions and behaviors while building self-esteem. It also offers some good tips for parents to help them communicate compassionately and effectively with their children. I really urge you to check it out.

My grandson, who is now five years old, was talking with me one day about things that were happening in his kindergarten class. I was excited about the fact that he is learning so much and said, "Leon, you have such an awesome brain!" He responded, with great enthusiasm, "I know, Grammie! I'm growing new dendrites RIGHT NOW!"

Research with snails has shown that even a snail can learn and unlearn behaviour. Here is what I believe: if a snail can do it, and a child can do it, and I can do it, you can do it too. Let's get to work and learn how to tame the beast. Why? Because you deserve to live your very best life, that's why.

CHAPTER THREE
It's All About First Steps... and Baby Steps!

There is a reason that babies learn to crawl before they learn to walk. Crawling is important to the development of the brain and is a necessary step in the process of becoming upright and independent. So too with alleviating anxiety: we start with first steps, small steps, and build on each successive step, until we are up and running. It is important to remember, though, that just as babies often crawl differently, your steps to curb your anxiety will be different from someone else's. You will learn as you go what works for you and what does not.

I recall a time in my life when I was having difficulty taking a first step. I was writing my Master's Thesis when I took some time to be with my mom, who was dying. She had cancer and had lived well with it for many years. As I look back, I know that being with my mother and other family members during this time was such a gift to me. My mother taught me many valuable lessons about living well, and finally, about dying well.

After my mom died, my dad and I spent a few weeks sitting in chairs, looking at each other, trying to figure out how to get through the day. There came a point when we both knew that I needed to go home and resume my life apart from him, and he needed to begin to figure out how to live without my mom. The two of them had experienced a full and close marriage for 62 years, and the task ahead of him was not only daunting, it was heartbreaking.

We talked about it and agreed – it was time. I trundled back to my own home across town, and sat down to work on my thesis. I tried to write. Nothing came. I walked. I sat. I walked some more. I sat some more. I stared at my computer. I finally talked with my daughter and told her I was utterly incapable of writing, much like being stuck in the muck. My wise daughter offered me some words of wisdom that served me well then and to this day.

She taught me that the most creative way to get unblocked is to simply…take one step. She told me to start writing about anything at all. I decided to try it, because I was desperate. I discovered that to *start writing* I would need to put pen to paper and allow myself to produce some random blather, because I wasn't capable of anything else.

It went something like this:

"La la la ho ho hum I have no idea what to write but Jen told me to simply start writing and maybe something will come to me, so here I go. Oh, yikes nothing yet but I guess when I think about my thesis, hmmm, well, I left off where I was talking about creating and loneliness and I was thinking…"

Before I knew what was happening, things started to move. It took less than a paragraph of nonsense before I was back on track. The process began to flow because, well, it couldn't help itself. There's some sort of law of physics that says that when something is at rest it will remain at rest, and when in motion, it will want to remain in motion. Once I started to make motion, the motion continued. I could write! This experience was, in fact, the origin of my daily mantra, MOVEMENT CREATES MOVEMENT. I will be repeating that one a few times, and you may find that it worms its way into your brain too. First steps, baby steps, right?

Wiping out anxiety is a little bit like that experience of starting to write. It starts with a choice, a choice to begin, even if you're not sure how. Following the choice, there is an action. Here is probably the most important thing for you to know about anxiety: you can choose to *stop* letting anxiety control your life… Or you can choose to *continue* letting anxiety control your life. But it will mean making a choice, and it will mean taking some action. Don't kid yourself – it *is* a choice to let your anxiety continue, if you do nothing about it. Did you know that?

How might you take one small baby-step today that will create change in your life? Let's focus on something simple. I'd like to talk about exercise for a moment, because often exercise is my first step toward change – making movement tangible. We now know for a fact that exercising regularly helps with depression and anxiety. There is an informative book by John J. Ratey, M.D., that you may wish to read called *Spark: The Revolutionary New Science of Exercise and the Brain.* Numerous research efforts over the past several years have confirmed the positive benefits of exercise. Perhaps the best way to confirm this for yourself is to talk with people who make exercise a regular part of their week, and then give it a try. Remember…thinking and talking about it will not create the outcome you want. Thinking and talking about it are two good first steps but the reality is, without the action of getting off the couch, putting on your walking shoes, and getting out the door to go for a walk, nothing will change. You will not feel better if you continue to lay on the couch. It is that simple. And this movement, this action, applies to making changes in your life regarding anxiety as well.

This importance of movement is certainly true for me. There was a time that I was away from my yoga class for several weeks, and the longer I stayed away, the more difficult it was to get there. I simply didn't feel like it. One day, I promised myself that if I went to the class, I could roll out my mat and lay on it for the full hour if that's what I wanted to do. I didn't have to move a muscle or attempt one single pose. I could lay there like a slug. That agreement with myself was enough to get me out the door and off to yoga. Of course, I did a full hour of yoga and enjoyed every moment of it. Completing that first session enabled me to move into successive sessions. Movement creates movement!

I have chosen walking as my exercise for the past several months. There's a park about five minutes walk from my home. It's a large, beautiful, peaceful area, mostly in its natural state, except for some gravel walking paths and a bit of mowing directly beside the paths. There are little hills, several ponds, some marshy areas, wild grasses, flowers, and trees, and the air is filled with the songs of ducks, geese, birds, and their babies. Because I have never been a natural enthusiast about exercise, I have had to train my brain to want to exercise. One of the things I do each morning when I set out about 8 a.m. for my walk is to remind myself, as soon as I enter the quiet park area, about how much I love to do this walk, and how good I feel when I'm done. That way, the next day when I'm tempted to stay home, my brain says to me, "Oh wait! You love this, remember? It makes you feel good, remember?" and off I go to the park.

I highly recommend walking as a form of exercise as it can fulfill not only physical needs, but emotional and spiritual needs as well. Being in nature is highly gratifying to me. I love the stillness and take the opportunity to do a little bit of meditating while I'm there. I have social interactions that fill me with a deep sense of connection and joy. At the very least I say good morning to several strangers (and their dogs) with an exchange of smiles. In the space of just one week, I experienced three meaningful encounters with total strangers. For the introverts among you, this would be a wonderful way for you to connect without having to dream up some small talk.

In my first encounter, I was walking with my grandson when we met an older man with a little girl – I assume grandfather and grand-daughter. From their appearance and accents, I would guess that they arrived fairly recently in Canada from India or Pakistan. As we approached them on the walking path, the little girl ran up to my grandson and I, smiled, and gave us each a flower. I was so touched by her gift to us and then somewhat surprised when the grandfather asked me if I could help him remove something that was stuck in his eye. I went to him and while he held his eye lid up, I put my face close to his and peered into his eye, looking for the thing that was stuck there. I didn't find it, but luckily whatever it was worked its way out while we were looking for it. An intimate connection with total strangers!

The second incident involved two Muslim women (wearing hijabs) with their four young children. We were all smiling at one another when I leaned down to say good morning to the youngest child, who was likely about two years old. The Muslim women were visibly excited about that. They thanked me for talking to their child while encouraging the other three children to also say hello to me. They were so eager to connect, and it just made me feel happy to make that connection with them. So many smiles all around.

The third encounter in the park involved a middle-aged woman who exuded kindness and gentleness. I often do some stretches along the way because I get sore hips. I don't really know why – perhaps arthritis. I find I need to be gentle with my body when my hips are hurting. Walking more slowly and swinging my hips seems to help ease the pain. On this particular day, the woman and I reached the bridge (my turn-around point) at the same time, and while we were there we talked about the stretches we were doing. I told her that I was looking for ways to decrease the pain in my hips. She told me this: "If you hold your bones and love them, they will heal."

As I continued my walk I thought about her words. I realized that it's easy for me to tell others to love themselves and their bodies, but it is also wonderful for me to receive this reminder from someone else. We all need to have each other's back. The bottom line is this: exercise decreases my stress and anxiety, gives me social con-nection, helps me to be physically fit, and connects me to nature. I highly recommend some sort of movement for you if you're dealing with anxiety – and even if you're not. When I take one small step to get myself out the door, the rewards are built in to the process and they are immediate.

Exercise also provides me with surprising friendships and the opportunity to keep learning. I once encountered a Sikh man who had come to Canada from India to visit his son. He invited me to join him as he meditated and did yoga early every morning in the park. During our first session together, he taught me some breathing to encourage my thyroid to function properly. The first few times I attempted this breath I sounded like a wounded animal who was about to die. It's a good thing I'm able to laugh at myself! I fully intend to continue this practice until I can do it properly, without scaring away the birds and the ducks.

If you find it difficult to exercise on your own, why not create a group of like-minded people for support? Research has now confirmed that when people exercise in a group, or with others who support their efforts, more success is achieved. I don't know any people in my city who are able (or perhaps willing) to exercise with me outside of a class format, and right now my schedule is not permitting classes. I decided to reach out to a group of friends via email to see if we might have some health goals in which we could support one another. Sure enough, there were about eight of us, from eight different cities, who had different health goals we were trying to achieve. The goals varied from weight loss to muscle building, becoming fit, or smoking fewer cigarettes, just to name a few. We formed a group called The Canadian Clippers, with the idea that we would clip right along to achievement and success by supporting one another.

We Canadian Clippers email each other once a week, some of us on Fridays and some whenever they have time. My emails talk about four things: successes, challenges, goals, and gratitudes. I share the things I have succeeded at during the past week, share what my challenges have been, discuss my goals for the coming week (and sometimes my long-term goals), and also say one or two things I'm grateful for. Not all of us cover that much territory in our emails, but the important thing is, we are all there to support each other in our efforts. We also share tips about the things we are learning along the way. If anyone has a bad day, or a bad week, the group is there to provide the reminder that it takes time to form new habits, and it takes time for our brains to create new neural pathways and thus new behaviors. I love my Canadian Clippers!

I'm going to repeat myself now, because this is important. You really do get to choose if you are going to be anxious or not, and then you get to take action to make it happen…or not. If you choose to learn how to be less anxious, or not anxious at all, it will start with just one step. One bit of movement. One effort. Maybe your first step will be exercise. Once you decide to stop feeling anxious, once you take that first step, something *will* happen. You will begin to learn how to meet that anxiety head on, embrace it, and eventually tame it.

Sharing Experience

If you're reading this book because you suffer from anxiety, I urge you to focus on the belief that there is hope for you. If you're the loving friend or mate or sister of someone who suffers from anxiety, and you're reading this book to educate yourself to be a good support to them, I applaud you. Or perhaps you are the parent of an anxious child and you are desperate to ease their worries. I have one insight to pass along to you that will be an important part of your support. Forget the idea that your loved one can "get over" anxiety by smartening up and having a nice change of attitude.

Perhaps now you're thinking… "Didn't she just say that it is a choice to be anxious or not? Didn't she just say that attitude is everything?" I did indeed say that. But remember, it is your loved one who must make this choice and embrace this change of attitude. Our loved ones will not get over their anxiety because we tell them to. They will need to make several choices in order to create this movement in their lives. Our job is to love them, support them, help them practice if they ask for our help, and do what we can to show them how we create safety in our own lives. I am a firm believer that we cannot change anyone but ourselves; but at the same time, I realize that if we make positive changes in our own lives, it is inevitable that our loved ones will be impacted, most likely positively, by the changes we have made.

You may be worried that you might do something harmful in your efforts to help. Remember, you are loving and supporting, not telling them what to do. Rodney Smith wrote a wonderful book, *Lessons from the Dying.* His experience is in hospice work and teaching meditation. I would encourage everyone to read this book, because it is chock-full of wisdom. I have learned from his teachings, and the teachings of many others, about the power of relationship to make a difference. I know that as a therapist, it is the power of the relationship between me and my client that makes all the difference in terms of making change. There is great power in the act of caring and listening without judgement, and great power in the act of trusting another human being with your most vulnerable self.

When it comes to helping your loved one with anxiety, the bottom line is this. If you care about him, you will help him by loving and supporting him. He will learn what he needs and ask for help when he needs it.

When our loved one makes the choice to work at it, he will need to choose to believe that it's possible to create change, and then choose to develop and maintain strategies that work for him. It won't happen overnight and it won't happen without him finding some understanding of how he became an anxious person. It won't happen without some awareness of what triggers him, or what scenarios are habitual for him. It will take creative, fully conscious, focused work to change his thoughts and his feelings. But he can do it.

I would like to say a word about therapy now. Having been a clinical therapist for several years, I am aware of the positive outcomes that can happen when two people sit together, one of them listening with an open heart and no judgment, able to ask good questions. It is inevitable that *something* will happen. Research shows that people begin to feel better after they call to make the appointment. Do you know why? Because their brain recognizes that they are willing to seek change, willing to take that first step. *Movement creates movement!* I love that we are able to now demonstrate this with scientific evidence, using brain scans to show that the brain changes after successful therapy; it's not just me and my clients *feeling* that it is true. Our brains have such incredible power to create positive change, and two brains working together – what could be better? If there were a band called *The Brain*, I'm pretty sure I'd be a groupie.

In any case, if you haven't tried therapy, I recommend you try it. If you don't connect with the first therapist or counsellor you try, find another one. It would be wonderful for you to have support from someone who fully understands what you are experiencing.

CHAPTER FOUR

Recipe for Success: 10 Must-Do Mindsets

I know from working with clients, and from experiencing this myself, that there are a few basic ingredients needed for success. Once you have the basics down, you can improvise and get really creative.

Conviction

- Believe that it is possible for you to significantly decrease or shut down your anxiety, once and for all, simply by doing the work. If you don't believe it right this very second, let me do the believing for you until you start to experience it for yourself.

Perseverance

- Be willing to persevere, doing the strategies over and over and over again, and then again...and some more...and then again. It takes time to train your brain and your body to behave in a new way – BUT IT CAN BE DONE! Every time you use a strategy, it will get easier to use AND become more effective. Built-in reward!

Education

- Educate yourself. Learn everything you can about anxiety
  – what it is, how it works, your own personal history and
  your family's history regarding anxiety, and the strategies to
  combat anxiety that have worked for others.

Silence

- Take steps to silence all self-critical, demeaning, defeating
  head chatter. This negative head chatter is gone, for good.

Encourage

- Be your own cheerleader. Do not shy away from congratu-
  lating yourself as you achieve small successes – because
  you *will* achieve small successes, and it will be important for
  you to focus on every little achievement. Your brain needs
  to hear about progress. This is part of the process of training your brain to think in a positive way rather than a negative way.

Ask

- Ask for help. Round up some people who care about you
  and are willing to learn about anxiety and support you as
  you try new strategies and begin to spread your wings.
  Learn who you can count on and who will not be helpful to
  you. Ask them to read this book, so that you're on the same
  page, so to speak. Don't ever be afraid to ask for help. You
  would be happy to help your friend or family member if they
  asked you. Many of them will be ready and willing to help
  you too. Not everyone will be good at helping you though.
  Some people make a great omelette, others do not. If they

are not a good helper, it doesn't mean they don't love you. It just means they aren't good at this particular thing.

Discern

- Be discerning. What works for someone else may not work for you. Pay close attention to what is working and continue to do it, expand on it, and celebrate it.

Positive Focus

- Think positively: Focus primarily on the positive (I know, it's hard to give up general and pervasive negativity, especially if you became acquainted with it in the womb). I am reluctant to tell you this, but if negativity is your best friend, you will fail. Detaching from negativity can be a challenge. It's similar to detaching from chocolate. But again, IT CAN BE DONE. The reward you experience will be the reason you continue to do it.

Seek Solutions

- Be solution-focused. Don't focus on the problem, the anxiety. Monitor your self-talk. "I'm so anxious! My body is going crazy! I'm freaking OUT!" Not helpful. Instead, focus on the solution to this problem. The solution is all about empowering yourself with some good strategies to tame that beast, and that is what we're going to do in this book.

Gratitude

- Experience and express gratitude. I have listed this one last, because this is, for me, the most important mindset. I'm hoping that if it is the last one on the list, you will keep it in your mind and start practicing gratitude right now. How do you do this? While you're focusing on the positive, focus also on what you are grateful for. I'll talk more about this later, but it's very important to be aware, every single day, of specific things you are grateful for. Writing them down is important. The words on paper are a tangible symbol for your brain, helping to make the gratitude concrete.

Now that you have the recipe for the basic ingredients that will create a nourishing experience, what do you need to begin to change your story?

CHAPTER FIVE
The Power of Creating
New Thoughts

To change your story, you will need to begin to change your thinking, and here is why:

If you change your thinking, you will change how you feel, and this
will change how you behave.

I'll tell you a little story about my own anxiety, how it rears its head,
and how I make it settle down. I have long been anxious when I
need to travel in stormy weather, on bad roads. Ice, snow, blizzard-
ing so hard I can't see. I almost feel physically sick when I think
about it. There are two ways I can tell my blizzard story.

Blizzard Story One: Thoughts and Feelings

This is totally insane. I've had a great time at this retreat, but I'm
really dreading heading home tomorrow. They're calling for bad
weather and worse roads. Snow, poor visibility, ice. I get so damn
nervous driving in this crappy weather. I have a little Volkswagen
bug. What could be worse than that? It's low to the ground, and not
very heavy at all.

What if I go in the ditch? What if someone crosses centre line and
whamo, my life is over? What if I get stuck in a snow drift and a

great big semi slams into me? My life is really over! What if I am completely lost, and it gets dark, and I have no cell service? What if I get a freaking flat tire, or I run out of gas? Oh my God, this is really horrible!!!

Result of Blizzard Story One: Feeling BAD

Now it's time to check out my body, and this is for real. My heart is pounding. My breathing is shallow. The front of my head feels tight and my teeth are clenched. My stomach is a bit nauseous. I'd give anything to not go out in that storm that *might* come tomorrow. Anything!

Blizzard Story Two: Alternative Thoughts and Feelings

Wow, what an awesome retreat we have had. I'm feeling really relaxed and I've learned so much. I love the people I've spent time with. I'm heading out tomorrow. The forecast isn't that great. In fact, it sounds like we might have a blizzard. I'm really grateful that I can travel in tandem with other vehicles. We'll help each other along the way.

I love my little VW bug. It may be small, and low to the ground, but it is mighty! It handles like a dream and keeps me on the road. It can really plough through lots of snow. I have my cell phone. I know that there is service, and if for some reason I have a problem, I'll call for help. I have warm clothes, and I'm a good driver. It will be a good trip home. Slow and steady. It will be just fine.

Result of Blizzard Story Two: Feeling GOOD

It's time now to check out my body, and again, this is for real. My heart rate is normal, my breathing is relaxed and even. My face is relaxed and my stomach feels fine (except, truthfully, I'm a little hungry for some chocolate). I'm ready to make that trip tomorrow. Yahoo!

Now it is your turn to try it, Story One and Story Two.

- Think of a what-if scenario that causes you some anxiety. Tell someone the story, with all its gory what-if details. Really ham it up, because that's what you always do anyway when you create catastrophe in your mind…right?

- When the story is complete, check your body. Where are you feeling the anxiety? Name it. Visualize it.

  Do you see what you did to yourself?

- Retell the story, changing the negative details and emotions to positive details and emotions, as I did. Focus on the fact that you are in control of how this is going to go…positively.

- Now check out your body. Are you feeling any anxiety? Probably not. See what you did to yourself, in a good way?

Remember, this all takes practice and perseverance. If you are still feeling a bit anxious and you need a little more practice, go back and tell that positive version of the story again, and this time, try to be more convincing. This is what needs to happen – you need to convince *yourself*, not me or anyone else. Remember, the thing you are what-iffing about is highly unlikely to ever occur, but if it does, *you will handle it!*

You can tell your brain anything – and it will believe you, if you are convincing enough. You can lie to your brain, and tell it negative, horrifying, agonizing, freak-out stuff, and it will believe you. OR you can CHOOSE to tell it positive, calm, peaceful, "I can handle it" stuff, and it will believe that too. What do you choose to do? The power is in your hands. The way you tell the story matters.

Yes, How You Tell Yourself the Story Matters

My nephew's wife, Heather Knoblock Cottrell, has experienced anxiety since childhood, but did not recognize it as such until her late teens or early twenties. She said that the anxiety became more than she could handle on her own after the birth of her babies. Heather had moved from the US to Canada, married and embraced a daughter, and then had two babies, all within the space of three years. That would be daunting for any of us, but for someone who experiences anxiety, the rapid, life-altering changes could be over-whelming. Heather sought help, and I applaud her for doing so. In her discussions with her counsellor, she learned about self-care, introspection, trigger recognition, and coping strategies. It was important to Heather that I emphasize, while sharing her story, that there is no shame in asking for help. I couldn't agree more!

Heather and her growing family recently moved back to the U.S., another big change in her life. After being at home with children, she was planning to return to the workforce, but her confidence was low. This diminished sense of confidence is something that many women face when returning to the workforce after an extended absence. It can be rather unnerving to get back into the world of adults. But Heather was determined, and to encourage herself, she faced the beginning of each new day with the same mantra: "Be brave! Be brave! Be brave!" She believed that she was positively cheerleading herself into success. But here's where it gets tricky, because our language, our self-talk, can increase our anxiety, or decrease it, depending on the words we choose while thinking about our situation.

I pointed out to Heather that her brain was in fact receiving a frightening message, likely to cause anxiety. By choosing the words, "Be
brave!" her brain was hearing "Danger, danger, danger! Danger
ahead! Must be brave because danger is lurking!" This would of
course set up all the appropriate physiological responses, preparing Heather's body to freeze, flee, or fight. What would surely follow
are the anxiety symptoms that are typical for her.

I suggested to Heather that perhaps her brain needed to hear, "I *am* brave." That way, her brain is hearing that she is in control, and she can handle whatever comes her way – the good and the not so good. If you try both scenarios for yourself, you will see that your body reacts differently to each phrase.

Daphne Rose Kingma, another wonderful author, influenced my thinking about how our reality is created by the way we use language. I often recommend her book to my clients and you may wish to check it out: *When You Think You're Not Enough: Four Life-Changing Steps to Loving Yourself.* The bottom line is this: our words do matter. Our internal words (thoughts) and our external words (dialogue) both impact how our brain will decide to grow. If we choose positive words, our brain will begin to help us feel good about ourselves, and the positive will compound. If we choose negative words, our brain will also be helpful – but it will help us to feel badly about ourselves, and this bad feeling will compound. If our word choices are of the critical type, we will feel criticized. If our word choices are of the more positive, complimentary type, we will feel more positive and more empowered. Yes, our words do matter.

In reality, Heather had handled so many changes in the preceding three years that handling a new job should have been a piece of cake for her – because she is capable, and she *can* do it. She had, in fact, been very brave over the last several years. In this situation, though, one of the missing links was this: she, too, had to believe she could do it, or it wouldn't happen. I'm pleased to say that Heather is now working and growing her awesome bravery. She asked for help, she was given help, she made changes, and she moved forward. She did it!

It is not just our choice of words, though, that matters. We also choose how we will think and feel about ourselves. Self-compassion is often lacking, or entirely absent, when we are struggling with anxiety. When that voice of self-criticism activates and agitates, it can be difficult to feel compassion and encouragement for ourselves. When the voice of self-criticism is the loudest voice in our head, perhaps it is time to relearn self-compassion. I say relearn, because I believe that all children innately have compassion for themselves, until life teaches them otherwise.

All too often, we speak to ourselves in the cruellest of ways. Is it any wonder that we feel broken and hurt? I urge you to begin now to teach your children that it matters how they tell their own story, every single story, every single time. They are watching you and learning from you how it will be done. The story that you tell about yourself is most important of all.

CHAPTER SIX
What's My Body Got to do With It?

We all feel anxiety in our bodies, whether we are aware of it or not. Our body knows that we are anxious, often long before it registers consciously for us. It is important to be able to locate *where* in our body we feel the anxiety, because this can be our first clue that we need to begin using strategies to calm ourselves. Once we are able to begin calming our bodies, our minds will follow. The beauty is, we will use our minds to do it! When people talk about the body/mind connection, this is what it's all about – the two working together on our behalf.

How do we find the anxiety in our body? There are many different experiences of anxiety symptoms. If you're wondering about your symptoms and whether they might be anxiety, I urge you to educate yourself by reading, talking with a doctor or counsellor, and sharing your experience with others who have been where you are. I can assure you that whatever symptoms you are feeling, these symptoms have likely been felt by many others as well.

Anxiety symptoms are caused by an overly stressed and highly stimulated body, and this has occurred as a result of our own apprehensive or fearful thinking process, or, much less commonly, because we are in actual danger, and we are being alerted to this danger. The physical symptoms of anxiety that you feel are not dangerous; they are not dangerous when you feel mildly anxious, and they are not dangerous when you are in full fledged panic mode, even though you may actually believe you're having a heart attack or that you're *going crazy*. These symptoms will completely disappear when your stress and stimulation responses stop. In times of panic, it is important to remember this. If you don't, you may find yourself having anxiety about your anxiety symptoms. This will increase your anxiety level exponentially.

STOP FEELING ANXIOUS ABOUT YOUR ANXIETY SYMPTOMS!

Let's use me as an example of how these symptoms might work. I've experienced anxiety in several places in my body. As a child, I felt it in my abdomen – either nausea or sharp pain. I occasionally felt anxiety in my legs – a weak, buzzing sensation that made me want to sit down…or fall down. As an adult I felt anxiety in my face – my forehead (maybe a headache or a fuzzy sensation), along with clenched teeth and tight jaw. Sometimes my lips tingled. Often these symptoms were accompanied by a nauseous, flittering butterfly feeling in my abdominal area. When I was in my 40s, I felt anxiety in my chest and throat. I was convinced that I was having a heart attack. I was terrified.

Some people get clammy, sweaty hands, racing or pounding heart, shortness of breath, tingling. Others may experience restlessness, a sense of dread, irritability, impatience, dizziness, diarrhoea, insomnia, irregular heart beat, muscle aches and pains, dry mouth, and so on. A few may even experience something called derealization, where perceptions of time and space are altered to the point that the world seems unreal, or depersonalization, where thoughts and feelings seem unreal, and you may even feel disconnected from your own body and your own thoughts.

We are each unique, and the physical symptoms our anxiety creates are also unique. What is important about these symptoms is to be able to identify them in your own body – and then visualize them in great detail, because once we can visualize them in great detail, we can again use visualization to neutralize them. I know this is true because I did it myself.

My Heart Attack that Wasn't

Let me paint a little picture of myself in my mid to late forties. I was running a successful company with a few employees. I was married, but my husband and I were unhappy in our marriage, for many reasons. I had one daughter. I was overweight from eating too much food and drinking too much alcohol, both being an attempt to soothe myself. I didn't exercise. I smoked a pack a day. I sometimes felt angry, resentful, lonely, and sad, but I put a smile on my face and buried all those feelings. One day, while driving in the country, sitting in the passenger's seat, I felt a strange pain in my upper body. It seemed to start in my neck, a bit below my ears, and it worked its way into my jaw, chest, back, and shoulder.

I should have gone right to the hospital, but instead I reclined in my seat, and when we got home, I laid down on the bed. I didn't tell anyone (foolishly) because I was terrified. Telling someone would have – what? Made it real? Made it worse? Stupid thinking, but then, I wasn't thinking at all.

After about 20 minutes of lying quietly on the bed, the pain subsided. In the days and weeks that followed, it began to happen more and more frequently, and finally, I went to the doctor. We did all the tests that one would do to check for heart issues...and I had no issues at all. No attack. No abnormalities. Nothing wrong. Except that I knew there definitely *was* something wrong!

More tests followed, and the eventual diagnosis was that I was experiencing "a spasm of the esophagus." I asked my doctor of twenty years why on earth this would be happening to me. She said that it was very likely a reaction to stress and anxiety. The pain had been intense enough and had frightened me enough that I began to think about making changes in my life. One of the things I did was to experiment with visualization. I didn't really know how to go about it, but I've always had an active imagination. I put it to work.

I tried to visualize what my esophagus looked like, and what it might look like in spasm. Let me tell you, it was absolutely wretched. It looked like a spiral-shaped steel vice. I furthered my visualization to include my chest and back. Everything in there was a tight, whirling mess, with rigid edges. I hadn't yet learned about the power of color and smell in a visualization. That came later.

Once I identified what was going on inside me, I began to visualize relaxing that whole mess. First, I would ensure that I had privacy. What I was about to do might be considered ridiculous by some, but I needed intense focus. At home, I would retire to my bedroom, where I would have some privacy, and be able to give the appearance of *resting on the bed.* At work, I talked with my staff and told them I was making a new "Gone Fishing" sign for my door, and if they saw that sign, I didn't want to be disturbed.

I would lay flat on the floor, in the middle of my office, as that seemed to help alleviate a bit of the pain. Then I would begin to breathe – slow, deep, gentle breaths. As my breathing continued, I would focus my mind's eye on the trouble spot – neck, chest, back, and jaw. I would begin to send calm, loving, healing, light-filled thoughts to myself – no easy task when the pain was so intense. The calm, loving thoughts were important because the pain created complete panic in me. I was terrified, and the more terrified I became, the more the pain intensified.

What amazed me was that a rather magical thing would occur once I started thinking and feeling the notion of calm, love, and healing. I gradually stopped feeling the fear. I would visualize the loving, warm, light-filled, relaxing energy entering my body, slowly untangling the rigid mass that was causing all my pain. I would think the words, "Jello. Jello." That sounds a little bit ridiculous to me now, but at the time, it worked. For some reason, the Jello that I saw was green. Remember… whatever works for YOU. In my case, I guess I wanted that rigid mess to be softer and looser and more pliable, like Jello.

Initially, the intense pain lasted twenty minutes. I have no idea why it was that precise time. It just was. The more I practiced this relaxation and visualization, the more quickly the pain began to subside, and the less often it actually occurred. I was stunned and quite excited by the power of my own thoughts. Eventually, after a few short weeks of practice, I stopped having the spasm altogether. As I began to get a grip on my anxiety, I realized that I was ready to make many changes in my life – and this is exactly what I did over the next five years.

My husband and I divorced, and we became friends and better parents in the process. I stopped smoking cigarettes, eliminated alcohol entirely, and worked away at exercising my body. I connected more meaningfully with the people in my life. I took on three volunteer jobs and felt immeasurably rewarded. My experience with anxiety created a tangible and life-changing transformation. I've since been asked how I managed to maintain the changes I made, and all I can tell you is that the rewards are built in. You'll see for yourself.

You Can Do It – Children Can Do It!

The beauty of using visualization (and the other strategies I plan to share with you) is that they're free and anyone can do them. For some, it's harder than others, but I guarantee that the more you use the visualization strategy, the easier it will become, and the faster it will work. I suspect some of you may perhaps feel foolish using this "woo-woo" tool, as my nephew would say, but in reality, there is nothing "woo-woo" about it. Using the power of your brain to feel better is nothing short of brilliant. Using visualization to heal your anxiety is a lot less foolish than allowing your own thoughts to create your anxiety. It is as simple as encouraging your brain to do positive work, rather than allowing it to do negative work.

I have discovered that visualization is a wonderful tool to use with children who have anxiety. It works effectively with clients as young as four years of age. You may wish to check out a book called *Guided Imagery for Healing in Children and Teens* by Ellen Curren if you are interested in learning more about using visualization with children and teens. It is also important to know that visualization works with middle aged and elderly people too. Age is never a barrier when it comes to using your brain to help you. Your mind and body will work together on your behalf. Let them do their work.

Grandson and Thunder

"Grammie, I'm scared of thunder." My grandson, Leon, said these words to me one day when we were cuddled up together in a chair, reading a book. In the background we could hear thunder all around us. I, too, remember being terrified of loud thunder when I was a child. My grandmother, Gudrun Johnson, was sympathetic about my fear, but determined that I would see the magnificence and grandeur of her Creator's work. One night, during a very turbulent storm, with bright and bold lightening, crashing thunder, and driving rain, she took me to the street, into the midst of nature's chaos. She insisted that I see how beautiful it was. It actually worked! I now love a good thunderstorm and no longer have anxiety about it. Exposure therapy (and a lot of love) at work.

But I am not Gudrun, and I wasn't about to take Leon out into the thunder and lightning. I have a healthy dose of caution when it comes to being potentially struck by lightening. Maybe my anxiety works the way it's supposed to – keeping me safe. But when it came to my grandson, I knew that I had another tool that I could use to help him, and that tool was visualization. He is a bright little five-year-old boy who loves to tell tall tales, so I thought he might be able to visualize.

I asked Leon where he feels the "scared" in his body. Did he feel it in his head, or his heart, or his tummy, or somewhere else? He told me that he feels the scared in his tummy. I asked him what the scared looks like. He thought for a couple of seconds, and replied, "Fish." He has a fish tank and is acquainted with how fish dart around erratically in that fish tank. I could well imagine anxiety in the tummy feeling like darting fish.

I asked Leon to take some nice deep breaths, showing him how to match his breaths to mine. I asked him to close his eyes, and then told him that a very special Fairy Godmother was coming with a magic blanket to lay on his tummy, and that the fish would quietly go to sleep after she put the blanket on. I gave him a minute to think about and visualize the blanket and the Fairy Godmother, talking him through the process of the fish swimming slower and slower and slower...until they were sound asleep. Then I asked Leon how his tummy felt. His response was, "Good."

Normally I would then have the Fairy Godmother get out her net, and scoop those fish right out of his tummy, because, after all, who wants fish in their tummy? But by then he was ready to move on to other things. It was enough for both of us that we were successful in alleviating his anxiety about the thunder.

Several months after our Fairy Godmother experience, Leon's mom and I were discussing the weather forecast, which had alerted us to an approaching thunderstorm. Leon was with us, so I took the opportunity to remind him that he could ask the Fairy Godmother to come with her blanket again, if he was worried about the thunder. You can imagine my absolute delight when he said, "Grammie, the Fairy Godmother has come lots of times to me, and she always brings her blanket. But now her blanket has the word *love* on it."

Oh, my beautiful grandchild!

While I was certainly pleased to hear that Leon had continued to use this calming visualization, I was even more deeply touched that he had taken our visualization one step further, a step that provided him with even more comfort. That one step was love.

CHAPTER SEVEN
Anxiety is a Many-Splendoured Thing

I found a poem many years ago that I thought described beautifully the fierce battle that sometimes wages between our shadow side and our light. At the bottom of the poem it said, "adapted from unknown author, Sicily, Italy." I read this poem, and it really touched me. I have recently come to think of it as a beautiful description of anxiety as well, and I'd like to share it with you.

The Dragon in the Cave of my Spirit

I feel that a Dragon has been using my Spirit as Her den
Her snorting and convulsions are painful to me.
And the pain has taken me to the brink
Of hopelessness.

May the Dragon leave my Spirit on a whim
May Her visits become shorter.
May I learn that She can be tolerated
    If only I can gain the strength to tame Her.
May my rescuers work well and drive the Dragon from my Spirit,
    With Creator's blessing.
May I understand at last that there was never any Dragon.
    It was only one part of my Spirit

> Sending to another part of my Spirit
> Urgent messages of my Wildness.

Whether anxiety has been with you your whole life, or it has reared its head suddenly, you are likely wondering what it is and where it came from. There are many components to anxiety, and no one is in agreement on all of these components. I'll try to give you a bit of an overview of the things that I take into consideration – the historical, the biological/genetic, psychological, environmental, social, political, psychic, and spiritual aspects of this interesting *thing* we call anxiety. I won't get too detailed for our purposes here, but rather will attempt to help you understand the complexity and, ultimately, the simplicity of it. Finally, as we grasp the simplicity of it, we will begin to diminish its power.

It is important for you to be aware of the origin of your own anxiety, because this awareness will be the first step to managing your anxiety. As you go through this section of the book, consider whether your personal anxiety is as a result of one trauma, or perhaps accumulated traumas, or whether it might be a learned behavior. Consider whether you have a long-established pattern of anxious living, or whether you are experiencing situational anxiety – the type that has been caused by a specific situation and will be alleviated when that situation is no longer occurring.

Historical and Ever-Evolving Aspects of Anxiety

In ancient times, we mostly lived by our instincts, using our mammalian or ancient reptile brain, the part that controls things like eating and breathing. Eating and breathing are basic, fundamental needs that we will strive to meet, or die trying. When confronted with danger, our limbic brain would spring into action, as this is the part that is responsible for our emotions, while turning our stress responses on and off.

It is helpful to know that within the limbic system is the important amygdala, which sorts out the incoming information to let us know if we're experiencing a threat or not. If a threat is on the immediate horizon, the amygdala will flood our body with stress hormones, in particular adrenalin and cortisol, preparing us to fight, freeze, or flee. Fortunately for us, the amygdala will also release glucose to our muscles to help us spring into action. Anxiety was, and still is, our body's most basic survival mechanism. We determine if the situation is likely to cause us harm, and we then act accordingly.

Picture yourself, a strong young woman out hunting the wildebeest – food for a feast that night. As you creep up on the wildebeest with your hunting tool, you unexpectedly chance upon a deadly poisonous snake at your feet, poised and ready to strike. Suddenly your body is flooded with adrenalin, glucose, and cortisol, creating the possibility of fight (grabbing that old snake and beating it, or flinging it far, far away), flight (running away from that snake at record speeds), or freeze (if you are utterly still, the snake might think you're dead and wander off to find more exciting prey).

When we matured as a species, our prefrontal cortex (the part of the brain that helps us to make good decisions and choices) also matured. It began, at times, to help us assess and react to situations. It also helped us to regulate our emotions and the signals the amygdala was sending out. Think of this part of your brain as the intelligence centre, full of important operatives, sifting through information to help us think, plan, and control our impulses. To this day, when danger comes, our body prepares as it did in ancient times to deal with the danger, but it now also has an intelligence gathering unit to assist us in even better decision making. Even though our body prepares us occasionally for danger that is non-existent, I, for one, continue to be truly grateful for the fact that our anxiety works to alert us to actual danger.

When we experience a threat (real or perceived), our body will go into stress response mode. Hormones flood our body, helping us to achieve the required physiological and emotional changes that will enable us to take the action we need to take to avoid the danger. Our heart will begin to pound, our breathing will likely be shallower, and our muscles will tighten to prepare us for physical action. There will be changes to our blood pressure and blood sugar, as well as our ability to see possible options of behavior. There are various levels of intensity in this response. Normally, when we experience a small perception of danger, we experience a small stress response;

a large perception of danger creates a large stress response. But when anxiety runs amuck, sometimes our stress response can be major, for a pretty minor situation.

We need anxiety in our lives, to a certain extent. Our anxiety prevents us from becoming embroiled in many situations that would not be good for our survival. We don't step into the street in front of a fast-moving vehicle. We try not to start World War III. We don't jump into the lion's cage at the zoo. Our pre-frontal cortex helps us to make good decisions in these situations.

How do we respond to danger? Sometimes flight is our best option. We try to run away if someone is about to stick a knife in us. Or we may decide to stay and fight, if we happen to have lots of testosterone, a few muscles, and some skill. Our third option is freezing, not often talked about. I recall a time when my daughter was two years old, and we became separated in the library. I looked and looked, called and called her name. I was becoming frantic. Finally, I found her tucked under a desk, in a corner, not moving. She froze when she became frightened. She was too young to reason her way to safety. It was in all likelihood instinct that told her that if she didn't move or speak and if she made herself less visible to others, she would be safe.

Let's have a look now at one example of threat or danger experienced in our society today. Women (and some men) are at risk of experiencing sexual assault. The same three responses can occur. Some women may attempt to fight their attacker; some women may try to run away. But for others, freezing is the response that happens. Women often feel guilty for not responding to this danger by fighting or fleeing. They may feel guilty that they were unable to move, unable to scream, unable to fight back. It is important to understand that freezing is not a choice. It does not mean that you are weak, or that you *let it happen*. Freezing is simply one of the responses our brain and body provide to us in times of danger.

When our anxiety runs away with itself, it can create havoc even when we are in absolutely no danger whatsoever. When this happens, we are experiencing a large stress response, when in fact we have nothing to fear. It is like the shut-off switch has stopped functioning properly. Our body and brain go into "Danger! Danger! Danger!" mode even when there is no danger. We become hyper-vigilant, waiting for the other shoe to drop. We begin to plan, constantly, for worst case scenarios, because we want to do everything we can to feel safe. At this point, our anxiety is not acting in our best interest, and is instead causing us great discomfort. We become utterly exhausted.

This glitch in the system can happen for many reasons, which we will explore in this book. Sometimes it happens after a traumatic event, where your world has been upended. You might feel that you can no longer depend on the status quo, that you no longer can expect emotional and/or physical safety. Trauma can ultimately challenge your world view, or perhaps alter it entirely. Anxiety can also run away with itself when, without thought or intention, we begin to repeat the thought processes and behaviours of our loved ones who have consistently demonstrated anxious behaviour.

Why is anxiety so complex and ultimately so simple? Let's have a look at some of the internal as well as the external components that may become a part of your internal fabric – and by internal fabric I mean the beliefs you have about yourself.

Biological/Genetic Component

Dr. Tim Sharp is a psychologist and founder of The Happiness Institute. According to Sharp, our stress response is influenced by epigenetics. Epigenetics is simply the way our DNA is manipulated when it is at the cellular stage. In other words, if the parent is experiencing high stress levels when we are young or in the womb, it is entirely possible that our genetic make-up will undergo changes to reflect that stress.

In my work I have found that, time and again, there seems to be some type of hereditary/familial connection, although it is my understanding that for scientists, the verdict is still out as to exactly how that might work. Most often when I work with a client who experiences anxiety, it comes to light that they have a parent, grandparent, or sibling who also experiences anxiety. How might that happen?

I'm going to be somewhat technical here for a moment and share a couple of bits of research. I think it is important to have a rudimentary understanding of this aspect of anxiety. Here goes! You've all heard of DNA, right? Well, there is also a thing called RNA, which stands for ribonucleic acid. The flow of our genetic information moves from our DNA through our RNA to proteins. For our purposes, it will be helpful to understand the bare bones on DNA and RNA. I searched for a simple explanation, both for myself and so that I could communicate this to you, in the event that you are a non-expert like me. As I have stated previously, I am not a medical doctor and I am most certainly not a geneticist!

Several sources on the internet attempt to provide a layman's explanation of DNA and RNA by equating the DNA to a cookbook and the RNA to the recipes within that cookbook. The recipes can be copied. This cookbook is one that we all use. It is not okay to take the cookbook for yourself because we all need it to live, and it's not okay to rip out a recipe either, because we may all need that recipe. Instead, what we can do is copy down the recipe and use it in any way that we wish. Our DNA (the cook book) is used to store information and our RNA (the copied recipe) is used to express that information.

I'm going to use my daughter and I as an example. She shares some of my DNA (we have access to the same cookbook). We have each copied our own recipe from that cookbook (RNA). Let's say it's a brownie recipe. This RNA can mutate, depending on its experience. Jennifer has chosen to put extra chocolate chips in her brownie mix, while I have chosen to put walnuts in mine. The chocolate chips and the walnuts each represent an experience or learning that we have had in our lives. The walnuts and chocolate chips will both change the taste of the brownie, just as the learning and experiences will change our RNA (the expression of our DNA). Jennifer may decide to bake her brownie in the oven, while I will bake mine over an open camp fire. Again, the taste will be different, even though we have used the same recipe. Now that marijuana is legal in Canada, I just might put some marijuana in my brownie mix, but Jennifer will choose not to. Our experiences of eating that brownie will be radically different, just as radical learning or radical experience will more greatly impact our RNA. My point is this: no matter what our DNA, our experience will determine how that DNA expresses itself.

Many of us, at times, have been very attached to our anxiety, and it's no wonder. We can become acquainted with it in the womb, and this attachment can continue for a lifetime if we do nothing to sever the ties. When a mom is stressed during pregnancy, the various levels of hormones in her body can become unbalanced. Her body is awash with cortisol. This excess cortisol can affect the baby's developing nervous system, and the baby can then become attached to it. As indicated previously, its effects can be lasting, unless you take steps to ensure that they are not.

As noted above, recent research suggests that even if you are born with a genetic predisposition to anxiety or trauma responses, your environment and the things that you learn can reverse the changes associated with stress by impacting the RNA. Studies have shown that cognitive behavioral therapies, yoga, mindfulness, and medita-tion are effective in reversing molecular changes in our DNA. This is very good news indeed. It confirms that we are able to change how we respond to our environment.

Although genetics plays a part in our experience of anxiety, we are learning that we need not be held hostage by our genes; our genetic make-up is only the beginning of the story. I wonder if it is possible that our environment is a bigger predictor of whether or not we will suffer because of anxiety? As we have noted above, genes are actually more like a code, a code that is dynamic and changing, a code that is influenced by our environment. When we experience a stressor, the outcome of that experience is going to be dependent on how we process it. How we process it is dependent on our environment and how we have *learned* to process it.

Continuing anxiety occurs when we have not learned how to process fear and uncertainty, or when that processing system runs amuck. (Yes, amuck is a made-up word. For those of you who have been feeling anxious about the fact that I don't know how to spell *amok*, I wish to confirm that I do, but I have chosen instead to use the word amuck. I want to remind you that your anxiety is like being stuck in the muck, and just as you can become stuck in the muck, you can also become unstuck).

One of the ways we learn to process our fears and uncertainties is by the way we are cared for as infants and children. The care we are given will program our neural systems to respond in a certain way. In other words, if our parents, caregivers, and teachers create an environment that feels – and is – safe for us, and if they teach us to process our fears and anxieties well, we will not be as likely to suffer from anxiety. If they do not teach us the skills we need, our anxiety processing system may very well run amuck.

If you're pointing the finger at your own parents, it is important to remember that this is an *intergenerational* situation. In all likelihood, your anxious parent was raised by an anxious parent, or experienced a trauma that caused anxiety. We are not here to place blame. We are here to learn skills and strategies and to stop the cycle of anxiety.

Another Word About Medication

Given the nurturing/environmental/genetic component of anxiety, you might wonder why medication appears to be effective for many. I have family, friends, and clients who have told me that they simply could not be without their medication, because it really does make a difference. I believe that it does, for many people. Perhaps the medication helps to sort out the processing system that is running amuck. Perhaps it produces an increase in serotonin that helps to decrease anxiety. This is definitely not my area of expertise, but I also wonder if maybe, just maybe, it is also the power of the brain at work. We are told the medication will help, we believe it will help, and it helps. Our minds and our bodies are interconnected in a mysterious and exciting way, and we have much to learn about this interconnection.

Leonard Mlodinow has written an interesting book called *Subliminal: How Your Unconscious Mind Rules Your Behavior*. Mlodinow has a PhD in theoretical physics, has co-authored books with Deepak Chopra and Stephen Hawking, and has written for television as well – MacGyver and Star Trek: The Next Generation. I like that he has lived a variety of experiences and find his books easily readable. In his *Subliminal* book he discusses research that was done to see if medication that was used to reduce the brain's response to physical pain could also be used subdue social pain.

Mlodinow reports that twenty-five healthy subjects were asked to take two tablets twice each day for three weeks. Half of the subjects received extra strength Tylenol and half received placebos. On the last day of the study, the subjects were invited one at a time to come into the lab and play a computer game. They were told that they were playing with subjects in another room, but they were actually playing a computer-generated opponent.

At first the game was friendly but gradually the subject was rudely excluded by the other players – an experience that none of us would relish. After the game, the subject was asked to fill out a questionnaire designed to measure social distress. The results were very interesting! The subjects who had taken the Tylenol exhibited reduced activity in the brain areas associated with social exclusion compared to those who had taken the placebo. They concluded that Tylenol could actually reduce the neural response to social rejection. This is fascinating research that affirms the notion that our minds and bodies do work together in mysterious and wonderful ways.

We human beings are intriguing and mightily complex creatures. The bottom line is this: If your medication *is* working, whatever the reason, keep taking it, if that is what you choose to do. To take medication or not is a personal decision, and I encourage you to talk with your doctor, and then make a plan that is best for *you.*

Environmental

As I stated previously, I believe that in many cases our "run-amuck anxiety" is very much a learned behaviour. Our thoughts create our feelings, and our feelings lead to our behaviour. You might be wondering how that works, exactly. Suppose we are looking at a situation with apprehension (thinking that something bad might happen), and because we are thinking that something bad might happen, we quickly determine how to proceed (we make a decision about how to handle this bad thing and how we feel about it – bad). Once we have made a decision, we will do something about the situation (we take action). Quite simply, we all learn this process from the people who influence us – parents, teachers, religious leaders, and even peers. How does this work in practical terms?

Let's take a look at two children, named Charlie and Jack, and their mothers who approach the world in two different ways. One mother's behaviour is steeped in fear, while the other is offering love and encouragement.

Charlie has grown up in a home with an anxious mom. "Charlie, be careful on the swing!" "Charlie, don't put too much sauce on that or you'll burn your tongue!" "Charlie, watch out! Charlie, don't run with the scissors!" "Charlie, I'm worried that you're going to hurt yourself on the..." Well, you get the picture.

Then we have Jack, whose mother is more likely to say, "Well done on that swing, Jack!" "Hope you enjoy that sauce, Jack. Maybe try a little bit before you pour it all over." "Good job figuring out how to get down from that tree, Jack. I knew you could do it." "You are capable, my little Jack! I love to watch you try." Now you get a different picture.

Which child do you think will become more anxious? Which child will perceive more situations as dangerous, needing utmost caution, thus reacting with fear? Which child will be more eager to try new things, moving more confidently throughout his life?

Or perhaps we have a little Canadian boy named Joshua who has two loving parents, enough to eat, some involvement in sports and music, good friends, and good health. Pictured next to him is Sami, who lives in Syria. Sami's father was killed after months of bombing and sniper action. He has often gone hungry, fearing for his life. His little sister will no longer speak. And he is soon moving to a new country where he doesn't know the language, has no friends, and no extended family. Who do you suppose will be more anxious?

Sami has encountered real danger and has had to respond to real danger. In all likelihood, he will need time, good support, and some experience in his new environment to encourage a rebuilding of trust and the retraining of his thought processes. He will need that, and more, to find comfort in the safety of his new home.

Or perhaps we have a little girl who has grown up in a home where alcohol and drugs are abused, and she has faced the unpredictability of potential danger. She is often neglected, hungry, and fearful of the violence that might erupt at any moment. Do you suppose, even if she escapes this environment, that anxiety will follow her? Let's compare her to the little girl who is tucked into bed every night by a loving, sober parent, one who reads her a story, hugs her, and tells her she is loved.

When we are physically unsafe, emotionally unsafe, or when we cannot predict what is likely to happen next, we will sometimes become hyper-vigilant. We will begin to focus on what *might* go wrong (what-iffing), in order to prepare ourselves for any eventuality. We will remain on alert. When this happens, we begin to feel anxious and we begin to act in fear. This is anxiety. When we continue to do these things long after the danger is past, this is anxiety run amuck.

Have you ever been the recipient of someone's road rage? A blaring horn, a shaking fist, an angry red face yelling curse words at you? Your body will course with adrenalin, preparing you to fight, flee, or freeze. Your options are to get out of your car, yell, and try to land a punch; sit there, frozen, holding up traffic; or drive away in great haste – possibly causing an accident when doing so. What of the person experiencing that road rage? Something has made her feel unsafe, and she is flooded with adrenalin, apparently prepared to fight. Not good.

The first time I was rear-ended, driving a company car, I was flooded with adrenalin. What did I do? I fled. The taxi driver who rear-ended me wanted to provide me with his insurance information, because he was responsible for the accident, and I absolutely refused to take it. I got in my car and drove away as fast as I could.

Sadly, I had to explain to the company I was working for that I had damage to the rear of the company car, a neck injury, and no person to pin it on! The worst part of this story is that at the time I was working as an insurance claims adjuster and knew in my sleep exactly what needed to be done after an accident. Embarrassing, to say the least.

The second time I was rear-ended, I was ready to fight. It was actually quite a minor bump, but I got out of my car and started to yell at the woman who collided with me. I am normally a mild-mannered individual, but my body was flooded with adrenalin, and I was reacting with anger and some aggression. In both situations, I behaved in a way that was out of character for me. In both situations, I was overwhelmed with fear.

Another aspect to our environmental anxiety is that in North America, as in other parts of the world, we live in a very materialistic society. We are driven by the fact that advertisers create expectations for us, telling us that we need certain products or experiences to be happy, implying that if we do not have these products or experiences we will be unhappy. If we do buy the product or have the experience and discover that it does not give us the happiness we anticipated, this can create a state of anxiety in us. What is wrong with me? What did I do to make myself feel so unhappy? I often tell my clients that if they rely on other people or products to make them happy, they are at risk of losing that happiness. The reality is this: happiness that has been given to them can also be taken away. We do not control the *taking away*, and this can often cause us great distress. Truly, the only happiness that cannot be taken from us is one that we create for ourselves.

We are taught to never take no for an answer when it comes to pushing our product or idea on someone. What used to be gentle persuasion and discourse has, at times, become manipulation and bullying. Never taking no for an answer is considered to be the characteristic of a good employee or sometimes a good leader. Is it any wonder that we are confused when it comes to allowing another person to experience their own autonomy? Is it any wonder that we often fail to respect them when they say no?

Fabrications and lies now often pass for the truth and remain unchallenged, or rarely challenged. Social media has seriously complicated this situation. We are much more interested in being wowed than in painstakingly conducting research at a fact-checking site. This bewilderment – what is true, what is not true – can surely create discombobulation in our lives. When truth becomes fluid and unimportant, where is our foundation for safety? Without safety, we will surely feel anxiety.

We crave to belong to an in-group, because that helps us to feel safe. Research has shown that we take on the beliefs of the group we are a part of, even though the beliefs may not have been our own, initially. Apparently just knowing that we belong to a group will trigger our in-group affinity. Mlodinow, in *Subliminal*, discusses how our subliminal self and our unconscious mind shape our interactions with our environment, and that when we join a group, our values or beliefs will shift to meet the group norm. From that point, we begin to identify the group's successes as being our own personal successes.

Just look at the American (and to some smaller extent the Canadian) political situation and the polarization we see every day. Each group member identifies personally with the success of its own group. If your group does not achieve success, you are likely to experience the anxiety of failure. You may feel unsafe. This anxiety is found in families all over the world. We might see one family member on the political right with another family member on the political left. Some family members may share rigid religious beliefs while another family member marries outside of that religion or refuses to accept the religious beliefs outright. There may be one family member who believes that anyone who is not heterosexual belongs in hell, while another family member is gay or transgender, either openly or in secret. The result? Much anxiety for all family members. The in-group has been threatened and safety is lost.

Our environment can create anxiety in our lives, but it is important to remember that our environment can also be instrumental in decreasing our anxiety. It's up to us.

Political

You may be wondering why I have included political as an anxiety component. The political is all about power – who has it and who does not. I'll give you a few little examples. We live in a sexist society, where rape culture and sexual harassment are all too often a part of most women's lives. As a woman, I have sometimes felt powerless, especially about my body strength and being able to protect myself. One in four women have been sexually assaulted, and I include myself and other women I love in that category. I am grateful to every human being who has contributed to the #TimesUp and #MeToo movements. This action is long, long, long overdue.

There was a time in my life when I would experience anxiety when walking alone at night. Great anxiety. My heart would pound. I would become watchful and excessively cautious. My breathing would quicken. Many women feel that they do not have the physical power that men do, and thus they believe they are at risk. Often, they are. Women then react in a reasonable way – they become hyper-vigilant, always prepared for the worst-case scenario. Sadly, it is appropriate behaviour for women to be aware of the dangers of being alone at night in our society. But when we are fearful *all* of the time, afraid of what is lurking around every corner, our anxiety has run amuck.

Another example of the political causing anxiety is poverty. Not being able to pay the bills. A concern about being unable to pay one bill can quickly escalate to wondering if you will end up on the street with your children, homeless and starving. We call this catastrophizing. There is a perceived danger, because the thoughts about being homeless have escalated from being unable to pay one bill to having no home at all. The daily grind of being able to purchase enough food to fill up little ones' tummies can cause great anxiety over a period of time. If you are not fortunate to live in a country like Canada, where you are assured of medical coverage, you might legitimately be concerned for your very life. If you can't pay for medical treatment, you might not get it. This surely would be a situation where anxiety could easily run amuck – for good reason.

War is an aspect of the political that much of the world must deal with on a daily basis – living in a war-torn country where physical safety, freedom from bombs, hunger, gunshots, and sexual assault is not a given, not any day of the week. I was talking with my Syrian refugee friend one day about how terrible it was that Afghanistan had been bombed – over 90 dead and 300 plus injured. I was a little surprised at how underwhelmed he seemed to be by the news. Finally, he looked up at me, shrugged, and said, "In Syria... every day."

What if you are born gay or transgender? How safe will you feel in not only the western world, where you might be discriminated against, taunted, beaten, or killed but also in the east, where you may be jailed or put to death simply for being you?

When we live in fear, we are anxious all the time. I know many, many people, not only Americans, who are feeling very anxious about what will happen next. Will I be the student who is shot at school today? When will the next war begin? Will it be nuclear? What about Russia? What about ISIS or the Taliban? What about North Korea? And what about a President who seems to have little or no impulse control? More and more people are arming themselves with guns, amidst the ever-increasing gun violence, because they are afraid. Fear run amuck. Anxiety run amuck.

Natural World

Yes, a word about climate and climate change, earthquakes, hurricanes, fires, volcanic eruptions, rising sea levels, oceans filled with plastic, droughts, and all manner of more severe weather extremes... all are creating anxiety in the people who face these disasters. Anxiety is about feeling emotionally, physically, mentally, or spiritually unsafe and uncertain. How devastating to have your home destroyed by fire in Fort McMurray, or perhaps one of our First Nation communities. Consider the uncertainty of the ongoing fires in California and British Columbia. It is likely that the people in all of those communities are now hyper-alert, ever watchful for the first signs of smoke.

Can you imagine living through hurricane Irma, only to be faced with the prospect of Hurricane Maria bearing down on you? The reality of Irma would create great anticipatory anxiety about Maria and its potential to destroy. In this case, the anxiety would be reasonable, because the reality is clear. But after experiencing two hurricanes back to back, one might begin to experience anxiety run amuck at the first sign of a cloudy or windy day.

I recall after the 1987 tornado in Edmonton, Alberta, where several people died and there was huge destruction of property, I would begin to feel uneasy every time the sky clouded over on a hot, humid day. To this day, I watch for the clouds that have that strange, greenish colour.

Snowball Interlude

My daughter, Jennifer, is always a good teacher for me. She doesn't suffer from anxiety, but she told me that when reading this section about the various components of anxiety, she began to feel overwhelmed and anxious. When I asked her to explain more, she said that it was "too much" and felt like a snowball rolling downhill, getting bigger and bigger, harder and harder to handle.

I can see how this might happen, especially if you are still seeing the anxiety as *you*, or something that lives inside of you, rather than a *thing* that lives externally from you. If you are feeling overwhelmed and can relate to this growing snowball, I would ask you to picture that snowball at a size that is still comfortable for you to hold in your hand. Now, wind up and hurl it against the barn door right in front of you. Whew! It is now in about a million pieces and cannot possibly harm you. As you continue to read, please hurl that snowball as often as you feel the need.

Are you ready to continue our peek at the complexity and simplicity of anxiety?

Social

Stress and anxiety can be worn as a badge of honour, especially in the western world where being an over-achiever is celebrated as if it were a good thing. "I'm a very busy man! I have so many tasks to complete that I'm going to have to work 90 hours a week to do it!" or "I'm exhausted! They say a woman's work is never done, and believe you me, I can vouch for that! I'm really starting to feel stressed and anxious about not being up to the task!" I am absolutely opposed to celebrating the "Type A" over-achiever behaviour. It is unhealthy and unbalanced. Yet, we do.

We also have anxiety that manifests in social situations. Extroverts love crowds of people and are, in fact, energized by them. Introverts enjoy conversation one on one and recharge when they are in solitude. Both can be comfortable socially, although in different ways. But people who have social anxiety are often not comfortable talking in groups, talking one on one, starting a conversation with a stranger, or making small talk.

I have worked with clients who suffer serious anxiety when simply showing up at school or at work. Blushing faces, sweaty palms, hearts beating like runaway wild horses – all because someone says hello to them. We don't acknowledge this problem in our classrooms. We don't teach strategies to help people with social anxiety. We don't practice scenarios with them. But we should.

Early in my career I worked with one young teen named Billy, (of course not his real name) who came to me as a last resort. It was a huge step for him. He was lonely and desperate to connect with his peers, but utterly incapable because he suffered from social anxiety.

We talked, we brainstormed, and we practiced. We used cognitive behavioral work to help him interact socially. We planned out strategies and then practiced them. He tried them out at school and when he came back for another session, we evaluated, made some changes and practiced some more. I wish I had understood then the real power of visualization. I am quite sure that if I had been able to do more to help him calm his body, he would have been able to calm his mind enough to use the strategies most effectively; he would have achieved the greater connection he desperately wanted.

Another aspect of social anxiety is conflict. For many people, conflict arouses huge anxiety. Why do you suppose that is? Well, for most of us, conflict makes us feel emotionally unsafe. Will he be mad at me? Will she still love me? Will he become terribly angry, red in the face, fist clenched, ready to swing? Will she think I'm stupid? Again, we don't learn good strategies for handling conflict. This is another thing we should be teaching our children in school. Parents are often not equipped with the tools to model good conflict resolution. Children learn from watching the adults around them.

Psychological (Cognitive)

This is perhaps one of the most important aspects of anxiety, because really, it's all about the brain. I know that I'm being repetitive here, but this bears repeating: much of our unnecessary anxiety is a learned behaviour. We learn to use our thoughts in a negative or positive way, and every single time, a negative thought will create much more anxiety than a positive thought. Seriously, have you ever heard of a positive thought creating anxiety?

We will be focusing in depth on strategies that will incorporate the way you think about anxiety with the understanding that your thoughts will influence your feelings and your behaviors. Enough said.

Psychic

Sometimes people feel a general anxiety that cannot be attributed to anything specific. It's a sense of unease that can't be named. It is different than what is commonly called general anxiety disorder. It has more of a psychic/energetic component or feel to it. There is a lot of free-floating anxiety in the air – people feeling anxious and sharing those feelings with their energy or body language. We can pick up on that energy.

Sometimes we encounter a person who gives us *a bad feeling* and that feeling is anxiety. We may be picking up on some of their anxiety – or, more positively, we may be experiencing intuition or instinct – that warning system we have, if we are able to tune in to it, that keeps us from danger. In this case, our anxiety is working to warn us, and it is working appropriately.

Spiritual

Spirituality has different meaning to different people. For some people, spirituality means nothing. When I ask my clients to share with me what spirituality means to them, some of them simply respond with, "I don't know. I don't think about that." But for others, it may be about religion and connection to their God, Creator, Allah, or Buddha. Or perhaps it is about meaning and purpose. Yet for others, it may be about connection to self, others, the earth, or connection to the Spirit world.

In all of these areas, we may experience anxiety. What if I have failed my God by not obeying religious commandments, or by losing faith? Or what if I perceive that my God has failed me, by allowing my loved one to die? In either case, anxiety can result – that old what-iffing again.

It may be that I am looking for meaning and purpose in my life and am unable to find it. Or perhaps I thought I had found purpose, only to be disappointed and let down. Again, anxiety can result.

Finally, perhaps I yearn for connection, yearn for closeness, yearn for an end to my loneliness, and I don't find it. The emotional safety, the emotional certainty, is gone, and in its place, I feel anxiety.

One More Really Wacky Theory Entirely My Own

Over the years, I have learned that creativity plays an important role when someone is attempting to decrease and eventually eliminate her anxiety. When I talk about creativity, I mean a whole host of different activities. You can be creative when making art, music, a garden, or a structure. You are also being creative when you are writing, cooking, creating a business or discussion group, or doing anything else that puts you in the flow of bringing into being something new or different. That got me thinking…if using

80

our creative abilities helps us to control anxiety, what happens if we don't use our creative energies? I wonder if this creative energy just sits there, dormant, unused or under-used, stagnating inside of us? What happens to us then?

I wonder…is it possible that when creativity is locked inside of us, and builds and builds because we are not using it, will it eventually become agitated? Can it become such an enormous presence within us that the energy becomes frantic? When this energy becomes frantic, is that the familiar "anxiety" buzz that we feel? Almost like we're ready to explode?

If we don't explode, is it possible that this energy will implode? It can't just sit and agitate forever. Remember, movement creates movement. If this creative energy implodes, is that heavy feeling from implosion what we call depression? Is that why anxiety and depression are often inextricably linked?

As I said, a really wacky theory, mine and mine alone, as to what may contribute to this thing we call anxiety. It makes intuitive sense to me.

Anxiety is complex, but only if we fail to break it down into three simple parts. The simplicity lies in first figuring out the roots of your specific, personal anxiety, and once you understand the roots, then determining what triggers you. When the roots and the triggers are clear to you, you will be able to learn the strategies that will tame your anxiety. It can be done.

CHAPTER EIGHT
Getting to Know your Anxiety

It is entirely possible that you have been feeling anxious for such a long time that you no longer identify anxiety as the "thing" that it is, but rather identify you, yourself, as being "an anxious person." It is really important to separate yourself from your anxiety. Remember, if anxiety is a thing you have learned to do, and you are no doubt good at it, you can most certainly learn to do something else in its place and learn to be good at that too. Remember the snail – if it can learn new behaviour, odds are that you can do it too.

Repeat after me:

> **"I am not anxiety. Anxiety is not me. Anxiety is a thing. It comes. It goes."**

Because this is important, I ask you to repeat after me again:

> **"I am not anxiety. Anxiety is not me. Anxiety is a thing. It comes. It goes."**

Think about those words. If you can truly separate yourself, the real essence of you, from the anxiety that comes and goes in your life, you will greatly diminish its power. Here again, we pay attention to the power of words. There is a difference between "I am anxious," and "I experience anxiety from time to time." In the first phrase, you self-identify as *anxious person*. In the second phrase, you identify as a person who has experienced this phenomenon. The first claims you – you are the anxiety. The second distances you from that thing called anxiety, and thus its power over you is diminished.

It bears repeating one more time:

"I am not anxiety. Anxiety is not me. Anxiety is a thing. It comes. It goes."

When Seeds are Planted

Where did *your* anxiety come from? We know that there is a biological/environmental connection. But what else is it? Is it something that has been around you all your life? Did you learn how to be anxious from an anxious parent, perhaps? Did your mother or father focus on the negative, or focus on fear, rather than focusing on the positive, on the "can do" instead? Did you face a lot of anger and criticism as a child – more downers than uppers?

Maybe you experienced a series of traumatic or difficult events, such as the actions of an abusive parent or ongoing bullying at school? Or perhaps you suffered a chronic or life-threatening illness as a child, or the loss of a parent at a young age? Did you suddenly and unexpectedly experience the death of your child? Was it one single traumatic event that upended your entire world? As mentioned previously, trauma is a significant event or series of significant events that pull the rug out from under you – in other words, create a feeling of loss of safety in a mental, physical, emotional, and/or spiritual way. Traumatic events that challenge or alter your world view significantly can feel like a huge betrayal. The world you knew no longer exists.

It is important to note here that the traumatic event does not have to happen to *you* in order for it to be significant in your life. This trauma may be something you witness, or it may be something that happens to someone you care about. In both situations, you can be traumatized. I often think that our news channels can traumatize us by the repetitive showing of traumatic events around the world. No longer are we insulated against the traumas that are happening far, far away from us. I recently cancelled two 24-hour news channels because my sense of well-being was askew. It does not mean that I care less about the world and the people in it or that I am burying my head in the sand; what it does mean is that I am being selective about the type and amount of information my brain is exposed to. I am still well informed and cognizant of what is happening in the world, but I no longer allow all that negativity to take root in my brain.

Often when we have anxiety in our lives, even though the danger from the traumatic event is long gone, the anxiety response can be easily triggered. A trigger is anything that propels you back to the event. It can be a sound, a smell, a touch, a sight, a song, a person, or even a taste. We may not even know that we are being triggered, but suddenly we are feeling very anxious. When the trigger propels us right back to the actual event, this is called a flashback. A flashback is intense and powerful. It is as if you are right there, fully and completely experiencing the event as if it were real. People who have been in combat zones, as soldiers or civilians, sometimes have flashbacks. Some people who have been physically or sexually assaulted also have flashbacks. These examples are only two of the possible situations that can contribute to flashbacks. The reality is, a flashback can happen to anyone who has experienced a traumatic event of any kind.

I'm going to illustrate my point by sharing with you the amalgamated stories of few of my clients whose names and story details have been changed to protect privacy. Charlotte was triggered by a smell. She was sexually assaulted by a neighbor when she was nine years old, and her neighbor was 16. He always wore a specific cologne (we'll call it Skunk). Charlotte was traumatized, humiliated, confused, and terrified. She told no one.

Many years after Charlotte left home and was far away from the young man who assaulted her, she moved to a beach town, putting her paralegal skills to good use at a small legal firm. She loved her new job and loved the people she was working with. One afternoon Charlotte was busy doing her research, feeling happy, confident, and calm, when suddenly she was in the throes of a full-blown panic attack, for no discernable reason.

This continued to happen often enough that she decided that she might be unable to continue her job. But before quitting, she thought she'd try one more thing. She would see a therapist and try to get the panic attacks under control. The therapist worked with her to determine if any new triggers had been introduced to her home or office. Charlotte realized that a new lawyer had been hired, and that he often wore Skunk cologne. Once Charlotte identified the trigger, she was able to work with her therapist to decrease and eventually eliminate the power of that trigger.

As you can see, it is often very helpful to identify the origins of your anxiety and your triggers if you can, because this will help you to develop strategies to work with it. For example, if your anxiety originates in patterns of negative thinking, you might wish to begin to work with your anxiety by working with your thoughts, changing negative thoughts to positive thoughts. Perhaps you will focus your attention on stopping the what-iffing chatter in your head. You may wish to work with the language you use in your self-talk or in conversation with others. Do you use empowering language or disempowering language? Remember, you can increase or decrease your anxiety by the words that you choose to use when talking to others, or by the manner in which you think the thoughts in your own head.

If your anxiety originates in trauma, you may choose to focus on identifying your triggers, and then focus on the notion of danger – and the fact that you are not currently in danger. This will then allow you to begin to calm your brain and body. You may begin to do what we call a reality check, asking yourself the question, "Am I in danger?" Then you will answer, "I am not in danger. There is absolutely no danger here. I am an adult. I am in control." We will discuss trauma in more depth, including a discussion of the things that you personally can do to help yourself, as well as how a professional may be of benefit to you as you come to terms with your trauma.

As you can see, anxiety is complex, but once you learn the ins and outs of *your* anxiety, along with some strategies that work for you, you will begin to see that it is simple, really. You can actually determine the place that anxiety will have in your life – or you can boot it right out the door. You get to make that choice.

PART TWO
Strategies to Make It Stop

CHAPTER NINE
I'm a "What-iffer" and It's No Way to Live

I see you. You are comfortably lounging about in your favourite chair, gazing out the window, and thinking to yourself, "What if I do such a great job on that presentation that they want to promote me and give me a raise?"

Then, because you're in tip top form, you enjoy the next thought that meanders through your brain. "What if I look stunning in that new red dress when I go to the party on Friday night? And everyone really gushes over how gorgeous I am?"

Because you're *really* on a roll, your mind wanders into the territory of your financial situation. "What if I can't spend my whole pay cheque this month? What if I have way too much money?"

Not!

What-iffers do NOT typically spend time what-iffing about positive things. Absolutely not. No, they spend time what-iffing about all the things that went wrong last week, last month, last year – and if you're Buddhist, last lifetime. What-iffers dwell on what is going to go wrong at this very moment, and what will most certainly go wrong in the future. Things will surely go wrong today, or tomorrow, or six months from now. Again, if you're Buddhist…well, you get my drift. You're most likely worrying about what it feels like to live the life of a slug, because what-if...

What if There Is a Scary Bear?

What-iffing started for me when I was a young child, when there were two especially troublesome things going on. I grew up in a village of 300 people. We did not have murder and mayhem. My home was safe. My parents were good human beings who cared for my siblings and me. I simply did not live in danger. But I what-iffed every single night when I went to bed. What if there was a scary bear hiding in my closet? I'm pretty sure the closest real bear was about 200 miles away. I'd never even seen a bear at a distance, never mind close up, and certainly never in my closet.

The second what-iffing was all about the murderer hiding under my bed. He was hiding there every single night. That murderer could jump out at any minute and grab my foot, or worse! He might cart me away and hurt me somehow. He might even kill me. I was terrified of the dark and all it might hold. Of course, the reality was that we had no murderers camping out anywhere in our home, at any time, for any reason. The odds of either of these things happening were pretty much zero, but both occupied my mind a great deal, and both caused me a great deal of stress. What-iffing, what-iffing!

What-iffing did not stop in my teen or adult years. In fact, it probably got worse. When I was 12 years old, nobody what-iffed more than I did about Khrushchev and the Bay of Pigs or hiding under my desk at school when the nuclear bomb was dropped. Later I what-iffed about boyfriends, about school marks, about body image, about career, about girl friends, and later still, about marital issues, self-confidence issues, political and social issues, business issues, fertility issues, parenting issues, and on and on it went.

The what-iffing was endless and also very, very exhausting. I worried all the time about making the wrong decision, to the point where it would paralyze me and I was incapable of making any decision at all. The what-iffing didn't stop until I had an amazing series of seven dreams in a row, and I began to understand what I do control and what I don't control. But we'll talk more about that later, because it's an important step in the process of letting go of the what-iffing.

One thing we know for sure is this: most of the things we what-if about will never come to pass. When I say most, I mean about 95% of them. Or maybe even 98% of them. The point being, it takes tremendous energy to worry about things that will likely never, ever happen. If that is the case, wouldn't you rather use that energy for something positive in your life? Imagine if I had been able to stop the what-iffing as a child and had instead used my energy to dream of inventions and create stories and plan adventures. Perhaps I would not have had an ulcer (caused by bacteria but aggravated by stress) at age 6 and again at age 12.

I expect you are now wondering, "How can *I* stop that what-iffing thing? I'll never be able to do it." I assure you, it can be done. I still work on it, especially on the days where my what-iffer makes a dogged attempt to rear its ugly head. But it happens about 95% less than it used to. I have about 95% more energy for the positive, productive, and enjoyable things in my life.

I'm not saying it happens overnight, or that it won't take numerous tries to change your thought processes, but it can be done. Let's do some brainstorming and come up with a solid plan.

What if...I Stop What-iffing?

This is what will happen: you will feel joy. You will feel relief. You will feel energized. You will feel that you have regained a measure of control over your life. That big "what-iffer" boulder will fall from your shoulders. DO NOT worry about what that boulder will smash into as it rolls off your back. It will find a clear path and slip gently into the sea. Visualize that, please. Seriously, let's do it.

Visualization: Choosing to Let Go

Close your eyes. Imagine you, with a huge black boulder of what-if anxiety on your back. How big is it? Where does it sit on your back? What is it made out of? Does it have an odour? Is it hot? Cold? Feel the weight. Is it moving or still? Is it pressing somewhere on your body? Feel how difficult it is to move forward with that boulder's weight. Is it taking away your ability to breathe easily?

Now visualize how it is strapped to your back. Is it around your shoulders? Your middle? Maybe even strangling your neck? Okay, we now have a pretty good picture of your anxiety boulder. It's time to take a step. Just one little step.

Let's create whatever works for you to break those straps. A Grandmother helper with magical equipment? A laser beam that will cut them? Your favourite Uncle Fred with his garden scissors? Hercules with a blow torch? Maybe you are wielding your own blow torch. Or maybe your helper is a wise old man with some new-fangled space tool? Or maybe it's Batman or Wonder Woman. Whatever and/or whoever works for you is the absolute right thing to use. You may find that the idea of a helper is not for you. In that case, visualize your own brain going to work to get the job done. That's the beauty of visualization. You are totally in control, totally the boss of your own imagination. Keep your eyes closed and wait to see who or what will come to help you.

Once your helper has arrived, with the appropriate tool, you are safe to begin the task of consciously making a CHOICE to let go of your boulder of anxiety. Ask your helper to break those straps. Trust that your helper (or brain) knows what to do, and that your helper will keep you safe and comfortable throughout this process. Feel the boulder gently sliding down your back and onto the ground. Watch as that boulder rolls down the path and into the sea.

Now focus on your body again. Feel the absence of the boulder. Feel the lightness in your body and the lightness of your emotions. Feel the strength you have gained by making a positive, healthy choice.

Do you perhaps feel a sense of emptiness where the boulder used to be? Remember, we talked about how attached we can become to our anxiety. We may feel a little lost without it.

Now is the time to replace the boulder with something positive. Perhaps a light Cloak of Wonder and Strength, or an Energy Pack for moving forward, or a Weightless Tool Box where you will store your strategies for being positive. Remember, whatever works for YOU is the right thing. You are the creator of your own visualization, just as you are the creator of your own negative thoughts.

Here's the beauty of it all. If you have, in the past, been the creator of your own negative thoughts, (and for sure nobody else was doing that for you) you can also be the creator of your own positive thoughts. You have the power to do that.

Just Say No to What-Iffing

The boulder is off your back. You go about your day, and before you know it, the what-iffing comes creeping back in. Of course it will, because your brain has been thinking this way for years and years. But just because it tries to come creeping back in, that doesn't mean that it is allowed to *get* in or *stay* in your head. OH NO. Because you are now the boss of what-iffing in your own life and you can choose to stop what-iffing right now. Over and over again.

The first step will be to recognize when you *are* what-iffing. That's not always easy to do but watch your thoughts. Be aware of words such as the actual what-if, and words that resemble what-if. As soon as you recognize that you are having a what-if thought, stop. Just stop the thought. If it helps you, imagine me screeching to a halt in front of you, with a big red stop sign, yelling STOP!

Once you have stopped that what-if thought, get your brain to refocus – on anything! Tie your shoe, take a deep breath, put the coffee on, cut the grass, touch your toes, brush your teeth, sing a song, dance, clean the cupboard, make up a poem, say one or two things you're grateful for – you get the idea. Change your thinking. Negative, what-iffing thoughts are simply not allowed. Remind yourself that what-iffing is a waste of your valuable time and energy, and that in all likelihood, whatever it is you are what-iffing about will never come to pass.

101

The final step is repeat, repeat, repeat. Every single time a what-if, negative thought enters your head, stop that thought, refocus, and continue on with your day. Eventually your brain will get the message. Clients have told me that when they begin the practice of refocusing, the first day or two they literally need to refocus what feels like a hundred times or more. The third day is easier, and the fourth day even easier, until refocus becomes almost automatic. I have also worked with clients who suffer from OCD, with one of the manifestations being intrusive thoughts. Refocusing can be very helpful to them. I have had clients who have intrusive suicidal thoughts. Although these clients did not feel the least bit suicidal, the thought of suicide kept popping into their heads. Refocusing, although hard work at first, was very beneficial in terms of keeping these thoughts at bay.

It is enormously helpful to live in the moment. Yesterday is all too often about regrets and should-haves, and for some, tomorrow is about endless what-iffing. There are wonderful possibilities in the present moment, if only you are there to experience them. I would like to suggest three books that might be helpful to show you how to live in the moment. One is *Look Before You Leap: 72 Shortcuts for Getting Out of Your Mind and Into the Moment* by Arjuna Ardagh. The second book is *Mindful Movements: Ten Exercises for Well-Being* by Thich Nhat Hanh. The third book is also by Hanh, and it's called *A Pebble for Your Pocket: Mindful Stories for Children and Grown-ups.* All of these books have exercises that you can do for yourself, but also do with your children. These exercises will bring you peace and be a life-time benefit to your children.

You will find that the more you practice this, the easier it will be to banish the negative, what-if thoughts, and the less often you will need to do it. But plan on that taking awhile, because it takes time to create new neural pathways in your brain. Imagine – the power of your own brain is going to be doing the positive work for you! If you are interested in learning more about focusing, check out Ann Weiser Cornell's book, *The Power of Focusing: A Practical Guide to Emotional Self-Healing.* The book is valuable in terms of teaching you to tap into the wisdom of your body, which, after all, is going to be important to you as you learn to control your anxiety.

Deepak Chopra, M.D., well-known author and healer, has also taught me about attention and focus. He wrote a good book, *Ageless Body, Timeless Mind: The Quantum Alternative to Growing Old.* He and many other teachers speak of the fact that what we pay attention to in our lives will grow, and what we ignore will fade. I know in my bones that this is true. If you stop paying attention to all of your what-ifs, they will not grow in your life. In fact, just like a plant, they may wither away from your lack of attention. Why not give it a try?

CHAPTER TEN
Control...and Letting It Go...Yikes!

Anxious people often want to control their environments – and by that, I mean control everything and everyone around them. They try to do this not because they are mean, or selfish, or want all the power. No, they want to control everything because they believe it will help them to feel safer, emotionally or physically or both. Sometimes we actually lose control because we are *afraid* that we will lose control. Sometimes it is our very fear that makes us most anxious and gives us that feeling of having no control. When we are filled with fear, we become certain that pretty much everything is going to be a catastrophe, no matter what we do, and when that happens, our worlds become very narrow indeed.

If this sounds like you, there are two important questions to ask yourself every single time you feel anxious:

1. Is this my issue?
2. Am I in control of this?

Let's start with "Is this my issue?" Is it possible that much of your anxiety is not even about you or your life? For many people, that is the case. My dear friend (we'll call her Lulu Treewalker) told me that she discovered that most of her own anxiety is about issues that are not in her own personal wheelhouse. What does she worry about?

She worries about her children.

She worries about her grandchildren.

She worries about her mom.

She worries about her brother's children.

She worries about the people at work.

Finally, she worries about everyone else's feelings, in most every scenario.

It is apparent that she is largely concerned about things that are not actually her own issues, but rather someone else's. When Lulu starts to feel anxious about others, a good question for her to ask herself, right at the get-go, would be this: "Is this my issue?" Because if it's not her issue, she can let it go. She quite simply is not in control of it. If she *were* in control of it, it would already be fixed to her satisfaction! But she is NOT in control of it, which means she will not be able to determine how things are going to go.

This brings us to the second question, "Am I in control of this?" Well, we already know that if it's not her issue, she will have no control over it. Realistically, what do we control? I'm asking you now – what do you personally control? The reality is, it is a small list. A small but very powerful little list. Here is what you control:

1. *You* – your thoughts, your feelings, and your behaviour.
2. How *you* respond to the environment (people and events) around you.

THAT'S IT!
YOU DO NOT CONTROL ANYTHING ELSE.

Think about it.

You control your thoughts.

You control your feelings.

You control your behaviour.

AND

You control how you respond to the people and events around you.

Did you know that you are this powerful?

Universe Hits Woman Over Head to Teach Her About Control

It only took me about 50 years to learn what I do control, and what I do not control, and the utter futility of trying to control things that are beyond my control. In fact, it was a series of seven dreams that helped me finally really *get* this. I was struggling with the decision of whether to move from Alberta to Saskatchewan, while doing my Master's Thesis. Things were not going well for my mom in terms of her cancer. I wanted desperately to be near her and my dad, but it would entail selling my home, making a really big move, and a disruption in my studies. My biggest fear was that I would make the wrong decision, and I felt paralyzed by my own fear.

Dreams are often my source of good information and inspiration. I asked for a dream that would help me make my decision. Since I was pretty serious about being in control of everything, it actually took seven dreams, not one, before I finally understood. The details are still vivid to me.

In my first dream, I was driving a car, and the car slid off the road, into the mud. Stuck. I had no idea who might help me get my car out of the mud, but I knew I couldn't do it alone. Suddenly a man appeared. He was tall, had almost shoulder-length blond hair, black glasses, and he was wearing a tee shirt, khaki shorts, and hiking boots. He approached me and said, "Don't worry. It's all under control." He pulled my car out of the mud, and the dream ended there. At the time, the dream meant nothing specific to me.

The next night, I had another dream. I was driving a motorcycle, and I went off the bridge. I was fine, but my bike was in the river. The same man appeared in my dream, and said the same words. "Don't worry. It's all under control." He dragged my bike out of the river, and my dream ended.

The next five nights I had similar dreams. I was really starting to pay attention. In one, a school bus turned over. Another was about a truck with a broken wheel, and so on. In each dream, I had a different mode of transportation, and each time, some sort of accident happened. Each time, the same man showed up, sorted everything out, and said the same words. "Don't worry. It's all under control." Still, the dreams meant nothing specific to me. I was paying attention, but I just didn't get it. Never in my life had I experienced a series of dreams such as this.

Finally, on the seventh night, the dream changed a little bit. I was sitting in the passenger's seat of a school bus, and the helpful man was driving the bus. Hmmm... This time he was actually in the vehicle, not showing up after the accident. It's interesting to think about the symbolism of the school bus – a journey to a place of learning. I love that! We were going about 110 kilometres per hour down the highway. It was dark out. The man was not looking at the road while he drove, and I was extremely nervous. Instead, he was looking at me and chatting. I finally said to him that I would stay awake to help him watch for animals on the road (trying to find a polite way of telling him to pay attention, I guess). He told me that this would not be necessary. I didn't believe him and became more and more frantic about the fact that he was not watching the road. Finally, I could stand it no longer. I NEEDED TO TAKE CONTROL!

I slipped over to the other side of the bus and yanked on the steering wheel. As I did, he slipped out from the driver's seat, and moved to the passenger's seat. I then sat in the driver's seat, grateful to finally be the one who was in control. I began to steer, looking up to watch the road. I was shocked to discover that the front window was completely boarded over with plywood!

I quickly looked in the rear and side windows and mirrors but could see nothing through them either. I was now in control, without any control whatsoever!

I looked over at the man, in a complete panic. He was smiling at me, ever so calmly. Can you guess what he said? I was not surprised when I heard the words, "Don't worry. It's all under control."

The symbols in this dream were a powerful teacher for me. I was having a great deal of trouble grasping the concept that in this journey of my life, no matter what mode of transportation, no matter what choices I make, it's okay, it's all under control. Even when I can't see what is coming. *Especially* when I can't see what is coming. Because really, things are under control – just not under *my* control. I finally, finally understood.

I cannot tell you the relief I felt, and have felt ever since, that I do not need to try and control things beyond my own thoughts and feelings and behaviour – firstly, because I can't, and secondly, because I can't. And thirdly, to be clear, because I can't. In reality, the true beauty in surrendering control is that we quietly get to choose how we will be in this world. It does not mean that we are relinquishing our power. Indeed, surrendering to the unfolding of our lives will empower us enormously.

After the seventh dream, I was able to make a decision. I realized that even though I could not see what was going to happen in the future, I would be okay. I could make a decision and that decision would be okay…because everything is under control. I did sell my home and move to Saskatchewan. I made the right choice.

You've no doubt heard the expression, "Go with the flow." I sometimes wonder why it is difficult for us to see ourselves as a part of the natural world. Just as the water flows, the sun shines, the trees grow to maturity and fall, so too are we a part of the natural flow of things. If we are using all of our resources to try to orchestrate our every move, we may well be overlooking the gifts that are available to us within the flow. And wouldn't that be incredibly sad?

How the Heck do you "Let Go of Control?"

The first step is to determine if you have any control over the thing you are feeling anxious about. Ask your self this question: am I in control of this? If the answer is yes, you can then make a plan, take action, and that will be that. What if you don't know what the best plan is? What if you are worried that you won't be able to carry out the plan? (Oh dear, two what-iffs in a row.)

If you're constantly what-iffing, a plan and eventual action will be almost impossible. Perhaps having a chat with yourself, over and over, to remind yourself "No what-iffing" will eventually open up enough head space for you to focus on pros and cons. This will enable you to think clearly enough to make a good choice.

Occasionally there can be another aspect to the difficulty of making a good decision. I often find that if I am unable to make a decision about something one way or the other, it might be because I don't have enough information.

Sometimes we can go and get that information, and sometimes we need to wait patiently for that information to reveal itself. If you are still having difficulty deciding what you want to do about the situation, perhaps it will be helpful for you to remember that no matter what you do, you will be okay. But in order for you to actually remember that, you will need to remind yourself of all the times that you have handled the situations that caused you anxiety, and you handled them well.

It is especially important for anxious people to stop and think this part through. When you consider all of the things in your life that have made you anxious, that you have worried about, a vast majority of them never came to pass. For the few that did come to pass, I would hazard a guess that you most likely handled them just fine. If you didn't handle them well, I expect that you learned a valuable lesson to help you the next time. Take a moment to think about this in your own life. We're not looking for perfection here. We're talking about survival, coping, and sometimes thriving. The reality is, you are alive and surviving, and this means that even your very worst day ever did not do you in. It's okay to trust yourself. You've got this!

And What if You Don't Have Control Over Something?

Now let's have a look at the things that you don't control. A few years ago, I learned a valuable lesson from my daughter in this regard. I was struggling to let go, let my daughter become the adult she was certainly prepared to become. It was hard work for a mom who liked to control everything. It was about the time that my daughter was choosing her post secondary education and her career. She wanted to be a journalist. Her dad and I thought it was really tough for anyone to make it as a journalist, and we tried really hard to steer her in other directions. I kept saying to her, "I only want you to be happy!"

Fortunately, my daughter had lots of determination, and when the time came, she studied journalism. Through this experience, I realized two important things. I realized that I didn't control how she would choose to live as an adult. I also realized that when I was saying "I only want you to be happy," what I was actually saying was, "I only want you to be happy the way *I* want you to be happy!" That was a tough bit of learning for me, but an important lesson for sure!

Let's have a look now at a few more situations to try and understand how this letting go works.

Situation One: Suppose that you are worried about your son. He and his wife are having difficulties, and you are concerned that their marriage might fall apart. How much control do you have over this situation? Yes, the obvious answer is, "None." The next step, logically, is to let it go.

Situation Two: Maybe you are worried because your best friend has cancer, and thinking about how bad it is, how hard it is for her, is keeping you on edge day and night. Again, how much control do you have over this? Same answer, "None." You should let it go, right?

Situation Three: The boss at work is a liar, a man without integrity, a fiend who is making your entire life miserable. How much control do you have over him? Same answer, "None." Let it go?

How might you handle each of those scenarios...letting go of the control that you don't actually have anyway?

This requires repeating:

Letting go of the control that you don't actually have anyway.

Think of it this way. I am not holding an apple in my hand. Can I let go of it?

No, absolutely not. We cannot let go of something that does not exist. What it boils down to is this: we are not so much letting go of control as we are letting go of *the misguided notion* of control. Let's see how we can do this, using the situations discussed.

Situation One: Well, my son and his wife are fighting. I'm not sure if their marriage will last. I have no control over that. But I can control how I feel about it and how I respond to their situation. I can use all the energy I would normally spend on worrying and trying to control things to do something positive instead, like love and support them.

I really want to be supportive to both of them, because I do love them both, and I know they've tried. Perhaps I'll let them know that I care about them, and that I am here to support them in whatever way I can. I'll ask them what they need from me, and I'll do it if I can. I'll let go of the outcome of this situation, knowing that they each have their own path to walk, and I'll try my best to remember that it's not up to me to create how that should go.

Situation Two: Meela has cancer. My heart is breaking for her, because we don't know how bad this is, and she is really struggling. I have to admit – my heart is breaking for me too. What would I do without her? I know I have no control over the cancer or her treatment. I can't waste my precious energy trying to control the outcome here.

What the hell *do* I control in this situation? Well, I control how I think and feel, and how I behave. I control how I respond to what is happening to her. As far as my feelings go, I'm worried, scared, and deeply saddened by this turn of events. My feelings are pretty understandable under the circumstances. I will need to feel those feelings, and work through them as best I can. Maybe I'll find someone to talk to.

As for how I respond to this situation, I'll let Meela know that I'm here for her and ask her what she needs from me. I'll let her know that I'm here to love her and support her, and I'll find ways to do that every day. I'll remind myself that I'm a strong woman, and Meela is a strong woman, and no matter what happens, Meela and I will get through this together.

Situation Three: It would appear that I am working for a man who has no integrity and thinks nothing of lying or undermining me at every turn. It's difficult to catch him out. What exactly do I control in this situation? Certainly not him! But I do control how I feel, how

I think, and how I behave, and I control how I decide to respond to him and this situation.

I know exactly how I feel – angry and helpless. Almost like a victim. What do I think? Nothing good, I can tell you that. In fact, my thoughts are going in circles. What have I done so far? Nothing. I feel stuck, and no response is making me crazy.

But when I free up my energy to do something positive here, I discover that I actually have a few options. I can talk to his boss, but I know that this carries a great risk of backfiring. I can make inquiries with co-workers that I trust, to see if they have experienced a similar situation, and ask what they did about it. Or I can calmly confront my boss, every time he lies, every time he undermines me, and see where that leads. That sounds like the best option to me. Finally, I can choose to stay at this job, or to leave. I am not a helpless victim. I am *not* powerless in this situation.

When we try to control things that we actually do not and can not have control over, we can become very stressed and filled with anxiety. We can actually start to feel like things are OUT OF CONTROL! Can you imagine letting go of all that and how good it would feel? It is important to know that there are several things that you can do to help you let go of the *notion* that you have control over something that you do not. But if you're looking for a magic formula, well, there is none. You just have to *do* it!

What is this "Just do it!" thing that I am talking about? It's all about taking action with our thoughts and our behaviour. Action will result in change. Action is energy and moving energy will definitely create some change. You will know when you take positive action, because you will feel it – you will feel it in your psyche and you will feel it in your body. You will also know when you take negative action, or no action, because you will also feel that in your psyche and your body.

Taking this action is a choice we make, and I would take that one step further: it is a choice we make over and over again. In every single moment, you will have the opportunity to advocate on your own behalf, to speak up on your own behalf, or to let yourself down. The choice is up to you. In every single moment, you will have the choice to let go of the notion that you control things you do not control – or the choice to continue to *try* to control things that you do not and will never control. You get to choose to let go. Remember this: letting go doesn't mean that you care less. It simply means that you are going to care differently and more effectively.

It is important to keep in mind that when you try to control the behaviour, thoughts, or feelings of your husband, your children, your best friend, or co-worker, you actually disempower them. You disempower them by implying that you want to control the situation because you believe that they can't. Sound familiar? The message they will receive is, "I don't believe that you know how to handle this. I don't believe that you have the strength, the smarts, the experience, or the character, to make a good choice here. I will have to do it for you." It's also good to remember that coercive control never promotes motivation in others anyway. It promotes anger, frustration, and resentment. Now I *know* that this is not what you want for the people you love.

What can you choose to do instead? You can quietly remind yourself, over and over again, "Let it go." The truth is, if you did control their thoughts and feelings and behaviour, everything would already be fixed to your satisfaction, wouldn't it? Remind yourself that you are not actually letting go of control, you are simply letting go of the *misguided notion* of control.

The issue of control over others is something that many loved ones of addicts will confront at some point. It is a hard lesson when you discover that no matter how much you want to control the addict's behavior, you never have, and you never will. If this issue is the source of your anxiety, I highly recommend Candace Plattor's book, *Loving an Addict, Loving Yourself: The Top 10 Survival Tips for Loving Someone with an Addiction.* Plattor is a Registered Clinical Counsellor working with addictions issues in Vancouver, British Columbia. You may also wish to check out Plattor's website and blog at www.candaceplattor.com.

She is well aware that addiction is a family situation and requires change in all family members if things are to begin to move in a new direction. Plattor recognizes that this change will most likely need to begin with you, not with the addict. She knows that when you are dealing with an addicted loved one you will, in all likelihood, be experiencing some anxiety and/or anger. Learning to let go of the things you cannot control will be an important step to letting go of these unhelpful emotions. Why not replace them with loving and supportive emotions and actions? Both will be more helpful to your loved one.

When letting go of control you may also need to remind yourself often that you are not in danger, that you are indeed safe, and thus there is no need to try to control the world around you. Certainly, it is our human reality that difficult and challenging things will happen to all of us. We may not control these things, but we can remind ourselves that we are quite capable of coping with them, especially when we ask for help and support from the people who love us. We have handled tough things before, and we will again, right? We can choose to focus on the problems or we can choose to focus on the solutions – the choice is ours. The first choice renders us a victim; the second choice is empowering.

We are all faced with uncertainty in life. We can accept the uncertainty (because, after all, what are we going to do about it?) or we can resist, fight, and rail against the uncertainty – a sure waste of our precious energy and intelligence.

Here's the thing: every person we love has their own path to walk. They have their own lessons to learn, their own mistakes to make, and their own joys to create. You may not be the boss of their lives, but you can most certainly be their support, their *person* – the one they count on to love them no matter what. From time to time, when they ask you, you may even be able to share some excellent thoughts and ideas with them about your own experience. You can empower the people you love by letting them know that you have confidence in them to handle things well. You can encourage them to step into their own power. When you do that, you will experience a great sense of relief that you do not have to try to control things for them. You can let it all go.

Once you let go of control, you can let go of control again…and again…and again. Ah, the sweet relief.

CHAPTER ELEVEN
Stop Stewing!

What should you do if you are thinking positive thoughts and undertaking positive actions, and still you find yourself stewing? A stew is an interesting thing. A mix of random but related foods, thrown in a pot, put on to boil and then simmer, sometimes for hours. That's pretty much what is going on in our brain when we can't stop ruminating about our *issue*. (Or someone else's issue.) The sad thing is, the end result of our brain stew is that it is never delicious, like the stew on the stove. The anxiety stew simmers forever, but we don't ever get any nourishment from it. If we do have a nibble, it doesn't taste very good.

Still, to this day, I find myself stewing occasionally. When this happens, I put on the brakes and hold up the stop sign. I simply stop the thought, refocus, and do something else. Why is refocusing so important? It is important because two thoughts cannot exist in the same space, at the same time. If you focus on *anything* other than your anxiety stew, you will be unable to focus on the matter that is causing you the anxiety. Think of it this way: refocusing is akin to walking down the sidewalk, encountering a barricade, and changing direction, thus allowing you to continue on your way. If you don't do that, you will find yourself standing at that barricade all day. This will not be productive, and it will not solve your problem.

Goldie Hawn has written a wonderful book called *10 Mindful Minutes* and I encourage you to read it for so many reasons. She also talks about the need to refocus and how she uses different little games with children to help them learn to do that. One is the Traffic Signal Game where Red is for stop, Yellow is for thinking about what to do (like mindful breathing or talking to a grown-up), and Green is for picking one of those things to try.

Hawn also suggests that another way to diffuse fear is to change the channel from the scary movie to the happy cartoon, first empathizing with the child's feelings and then helping them think of something fun to do.

I know from experience that stewing and what-iffing will NOT change the outcome of the situation I am worried about. Probably what has helped me the most with this stop stewing situation is the understanding that if I *could* control what is going on, I would have fixed it already. But **I cannot control what I do not control**! It takes practice and more practice and more practice, but eventually the time it takes to recognize stewing and to then stop stewing gets shorter and shorter, until it almost becomes automatic.

Bedtime Stew

Some people do their best stewing at night while they are in bed. A good thought to remember is this: never in a million gazillion years has a problem been solved at night while you are in bed, stewing away. Laying there stewing about things you have no control over will not yield productive results. Maybe you will get some good answers in your dreams, but that won't happen while you're awake and what-iffing.

The simple reality is this: if we really work at mindful focusing and refocusing, we will have more control over what we focus on generally. We will have this control because we are growing new neural pathways in our brain. It will quite simply get easier and easier to steer our focus in a positive direction. Using concrete symbols such as traffic lights, television channels or sidewalk blockades will help our brain get the picture a little sooner. It is for this reason that I suggest to clients that they create a Stewing Pot to place by their bed at night. They can use a container (like a teapot with a lid) that they have at home, or go to the Dollar Store to buy a small box with a lid. If they are handy, they might build a small wooden or metal box with a lid. Or use an old jewelry box. But this box *must* have a lid. Whatever you have on hand or can create will work!

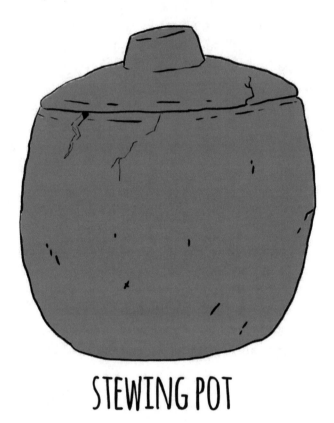

STEWING POT

I suggest that clients also bring to the bedroom, along with the Stewing Pot, a small pad of paper and a pen. Then when the stewing starts, and when the what-iffing rears its head, take a moment to write down the worry on the paper, put it in the box, and put the lid on the box. The next step is to then agree with yourself that just for tonight, there will be no worrying about this particular issue. By putting the worry down on paper, you take it out of your brain. By putting that paper in the box, and putting the lid on the box, you are telling your brain... this is shut down for tonight. Over. Done.

You can remind yourself that if it is absolutely necessary, you can take the worry out of the box in the morning, and stew away. (Chances are, you won't need to do that.) Every single time a worry comes, repeat, repeat, repeat, until all the worries are in the box. Good night, sleep tight.

CHAPTER TWELVE
Giving Anxiety a Break

You might be wondering why, if you intend to go into battle with this thing called anxiety, that I am now suggesting you give it a break. My thinking is this: when we think angry and fearful thoughts, we tend to lose control. When we think loving and calm thoughts, we tend to maintain control. Why not use the same thinking with our anxiety?

Remember how we talked about anxiety as being a "thing" and not being *you?* Let's visualize your anxiety as the thing, over there, in its own little box, separate from you. Now let's visualize the thing moving towards you, as it sometimes does. Now visualize yourself feeling agitated about this. Your agitation is increasing… and increasing…and before you know it, you're trying to kill that little anxiety box, or at least render it powerless in a hurry. You are jumping up and down and screeching and smashing it with a hammer, being a total psycho, really. But look at it – you're not even making a dent! In fact, it's growing. Now, do you feel better? No, I think not.

Now visualize that little box of anxiety coming towards you. Take a nice, deep breath, and calmly say to yourself, "Oh, here comes a little bit of anxiety. It comes, it goes. I know that, because it happens every single time. It comes, it goes. Okay, I am going to experience a little bit of anxiety now. Good thing I've learned a lot of strategies to help me out. I will simply allow this thing to do its thing, and then it will be over." You might even want to give that anxiety a friendly little pat on the head, just to show it who's boss.

How do you feel now? I'm thinking that you are actually feeling quite calm. I know my body certainly reacted to both scenarios quite differently, and I expect yours did too. The first scenario reeks of, "Danger! Danger! Danger!" while the second creates a much greater sense of calm and safety.

We stand a better chance of controlling our anxiety if we befriend it and simply allow it to happen. We allow it to happen, knowing that we have strategies to systematically begin to reduce the level of intensity and duration. We allow our brain to do the work for us. We make the most of the creative, problem-solving part of our brain.

What's a Number or Label Got to Do with It?

Some people find it effective to number their anxiety on a scale of one to ten. This can be helpful for a couple of reasons. By giving it a number, you will be paying attention to the fact that you ARE experiencing anxiety, which is important. If you can catch your anxiety at a lower intensity, and begin to use your strategies right away, there is a good possibility that it will not become very intense. Secondly, by numbering the intensity of what you are feeling, you will be able to track not only how intense it is, but also track the decreasing intensity – and this is important for your brain to note. Pay attention to success, right? But to do this numbering, you first need to know where you experience anxiety in your body, and then be able to identify it when it is happening. As discussed previously, you can't work with something that you don't recognize.

Let's take a minute to discover where you experience anxiety in your body, and what it feels like. Conjure up a fairly mild scenario that gives you anxiety. Use all the powers of your visualization to find it in your body. Is it in your chest, or your forehead, or your stomach? See its shape. Is it a black blob, or zig-zaggy sharp marks, or does it look like bilious sludge? Maybe it even looks like a lion or a thundercloud. What color is it? Does it have an odor? Is it moving or still? Does it appear to be young or old?

If you've been successful conjuring up a mild bit of anxiety (which I'm sure you're good at) and identified where in your body this anxiety is located, what it looks like, smells like, and feels like, you will perhaps be ready to give it a number. Is it a three? A four? A six? If it's higher than a six, you did *too* good of a job conjuring up the anxiety. Compare it to your worst-case anxiety, which will be a ten (and I know you just said to yourself that yours is WAY higher than a ten! I know that because that's what we anxious humans do). I'm laughing with great compassion, and I hope that by now, you are laughing with me, having compassion for yourself.

Now take that number, perhaps the four, and practice a strategy. Let's use visualization this time. Summon your Fairy Godmother, or Superhero, or Grandmother, or Wise Woman, or whoever it is you have decided to have as your helper and let them do their magic.

Perhaps they will send laser beams of light to slowly disintegrate the anxiety, or maybe your helper will have a magic blanket to lay over the frenzied area, to slowly bring everything to a state of stillness. If you find that the idea of a helper is simply too silly for you, visualize your very own brain, and the power of its capability to help you with this. Imagine it doing its thing.

Really focus for a minute on this, taking nice, deep, easy breaths. Think the words, "Slow down" as you breathe in and out. Now return your focus to your helper and her work. Be aware of your self-talk. Are you being critical or skeptical of the possibilities? Are you doubting the power of your own brain? Watch your helper work as the shape of your anxiety begins to change. Notice how the movement begins to slow down. See how the image of your anxiety begins to fade. Be aware of the lessening of pain or nausea in that area. Once your helper has done her job, you will experience a sense of calm. When this happens, give your feeling another number. Are you at a one or two? Excellent!

The next step is to congratulate yourself, because you have been able to reduce the intensity of your anxiety, and your brain needs to hear that success has been achieved. We are working to establish new neural pathways, and your brain is human after all – it likes to feel successful too! I would suggest that you practice this several times, and always use it the minute you begin to detect some anxiety in your body. Often you will feel the anxiety in your body before your mind becomes aware of it. In this case, your body is your ally. It will help you identify the anxiety and make way for your brain to begin to work on the task.

Don't worry that you are an old dog who cannot learn new tricks, or that you've had anxiety for so many years you must be a hopeless case. We now know that our brain can grow new neurons and create new neural pathways any time we have a new experience, and we know that this occurs throughout our lifetime. It seems to me that it is another gift that keeps on giving, because growing new neural pathways after learning something new is going to create the desire for more learning, is it not? Even if you are *really* old, you can keep having new experiences and learning new things.

I don't consider myself to be an old dog quite yet, but the other day I had an interesting conversation with my grandson. He asked me if my mom let me spend a lot of time on the computer when I was a little girl. I said, "No, Leon. There were no computers when I was a little girl." He seemed to be very surprised by that, and with all the gravity that a five-year-old can muster, he asked, "Was it the Stone Age then, Grammie?"

If you are part of the Stone Age, or simply interested in understanding more about life-long learning, you may enjoy Daniel Siegel's book, *Mindsight: Transform your Brain with the New Science of Kindness,* and Gene Cohen's book, *The Mature Mind: The Positive Power of the Aging Brain.* Both will do a great job in assuring you that you do have the capability to learn new tricks!

Anxiety and Procrastination

Often people who deal with anxiety are chronic procrastinators. It is a misguided notion that if you avoid what is making you anxious, it will go away, or it will feel less worrisome. I know that your thinking brain knows this is not logical. Why would you not challenge that thought, and instead behave as if it were true? Your procrastination is most likely about fear, and by avoiding what makes you afraid, you believe that you will feel safe. I hazard a guess that this is all going on at the subconscious level because if you think it through logically, you will know it's not true. Knowing this, you now have another strategy to practice: never, ever put off doing what you are feeling anxious about. I can guarantee you that it will not get easier, and in fact it will only become much more difficult.

I have watched people deal with fears and phobias on *The Amazing Race*, and if you watch the show, you will be familiar with the ways in which the contestants handle their fear. One example of such a fear is when a racer is afraid of heights. This problem is invariably tackled in one of two ways. The first is the racer who sits on the ground, cries, says something like "I can't do it! I can't do it!" and sometimes ends up taking the penalty. The second type of racer is the one who states clearly, in various ways, that they are terrified, that they have a fear of heights, and that they would rather eat dirt than do this thing – and then they get up there, close their eyes, and give it a go. Most often, once the deed is done, the racer is greatly relieved and quite proud of the accomplishment!

Or perhaps you are a perfectionist. Did I say perhaps? Many people who have anxiety are perfectionists to some degree or other. Again, the fear of not doing it correctly, the never ending what-iffing. Paralyzing, right?

Let's talk about John for a minute. He loves to be a handy kind of guy, but he is such a perfectionist that it's hard for him to produce something he feels good about. He constantly criticizes himself and the work he is doing, sometimes to the point where he can't even get started, because it's simply not going to be good enough. What does he do instead? He procrastinates. His wife is upset with him because the kitchen renovations have turned the house upside down for the past 11 months.

Rather than actually starting the project, he goes golfing. Then he watches the game on TV, and then he mows the grass, and then he stops to have a beer. His wife is becoming angrier and more frustrated with each passing moment. In no time at all, it's Monday, and well, he can't get it done on a work day, can he? Does putting the job off make it easier or harder for him to get this done? If you're a procrastinator, you know the answer to that one.

It's often difficult for anxious people to say, "This is good enough. I am good enough." We are right back at fear, once again. The fear of judgment, the fear that we will be found lacking, and when we believe that we have been judged, and found lacking, we do not feel emotionally safe. What, then, will help us begin to move through our fear?

Taking one step.

It is vitally important to believe that taking that one step will be worth our while. To help you take this one step, it is important that you believe that you have something valuable to gain. Why do something if it is of no benefit to you? You are likely aware that what you are going through now, with your over-the-top, out of control anxiety, cannot in any universe be better than the alternative, which is to take one step, and then another, to do something about it. You are also likely aware that if you do not take that step, your painful anxiety will keep coming at you, relentlessly. The first scenario, doing nothing, is a never ending black hole that gets deeper and deeper; the second scenario, taking one step, is the first step of an amazing and joyful journey. Remember, movement creates movement!

In other words, jump in and get it done. What's the worst that can happen? Certainly, it cannot be as bad as you have imagined in your own mind.

We can use me as an example for what not to do when it comes to procrastination. When I was young, I actually enjoyed public speaking. Not the spontaneous, off the cuff public speaking, but the "I have prepared a speech and I know it inside and out" kind of public speaking. Then for many years, I did no speaking in public of any kind. Finally, the day came when I was asked to give a talk. I was absolutely terrified, and tried to do everything in my power to get out of giving this talk. The more I tried in my mind to get out of it, the worse it became. The self-talk? I wouldn't speak to my worst enemy the way I was speaking to myself. But more on self-talk later.

Try as I might to avoid this speech, it was no dice, as my father would say; I had to give that speech. I made my way to the front of the room. My hands and legs were shaking, my dry mouth seemed to be filled with a gluey paste. My heart was pounding. I was embarrassed to be standing in front of a group of my peers, trying to give this talk, because I was such a wretched mess.

As I faced my audience I had an unexpected revelation: I realized that everyone in that room knew I was a mess, including me. I had nothing to lose. I decided to state the obvious. Remember the strategy about asking for help, rallying your resources? I explained to my audience at the outset that it had been some time since I had done any public speaking, and that I was feeling very nervous, but that I would do my best. Basically, I was asking for the audience to help me, to support me, with kindness. And you know what? They did! The whole room gave me smiles and looks of encouragement. I took a deep breath and began to talk. It went well.

I learned a couple of lessons here. One was about procrastination, and how it only intensifies the problem. The other was about doing a reality check. From that day forward, I would remind myself that I am quite capable of speaking in public, and that there is really no reason to get my knickers in a knot. I would also remind myself that not even once have I upchucked over the entire front row, or peed my pants. In fact, I am usually happy with the job I do and enjoy doing it. Having this conscious awareness of the *reality* of the situation has served me well on many occasions.

The Awesome Value of a Reality Check

We've already discussed how our anxiety is often not based in reality, but rather at the root of it is the what-iffing, the negative thinking, and the catastrophizing. Because of this, doing continual reality checks can be an invaluable strategy to lessen the intensity of your anxiety.

To do a reality check, we might begin with this question. "How many times in the past has this (worst case scenario you're fretting over) actually happened to me?"

The answer to this question is usually "None." That should tell you something right there. If it has never happened to you in the past, what is the likelihood of it happening now or in the future? Probably none. We don't worry anymore about things that are not likely to happen, right? Good! End of worrying about that one. NO WHAT-IFFING!

If, when you do your reality check, you discover that this worst thing actually did happen once before, it is time to ask another question: "How did I handle it?" If you handled it well, stop worrying. If you didn't, start brainstorming as to how you might handle it better. Rally your resources. Ask for help. Make a plan. Always remember that you are capable of handling whatever comes your way. To repeat the blurb that I love..."**You have survived 100% of your worst days. You are just fine.**"

CHAPTER THIRTEEN
Anxiety and Trauma

We have discussed briefly how trauma is sometimes at the root of anxiety. Let's suppose that your life has been one of safety, belonging, acceptance, and love. A good life, one that is not filled with fear. But one day, when you were least expecting it, something traumatic occurred; a sudden death, perhaps, or physical assault. Maybe you were at a music event (or in your classroom) when an assailant started shooting at everyone. Or perhaps your life has been filled with traumatic experiences such as negligence, physical or sexual abuse, domestic violence, or illness. Or maybe you are a soldier and you have experienced a series of traumatic events while serving your country.

Perhaps you experienced trauma in the Residential School system or during the Sixties Scoop. In both situations Indigenous children were removed, often forcibly, from their parents and their homes and systematically stripped of their language, culture, appearance, traditions, and spiritual beliefs. Maybe you are the parent whose children were taken from you. The intergenerational trauma that occurred because of this shameful time in Canada's history continues to this day. These life experiences can surely instigate an anxiety response or much worse.

Much of what I initially learned about trauma I learned from Jane Simington, Ph.D., who works with sufferers and survivors of trauma and grief, and trains other professionals and semi-professionals to do this work as well, through her company Taking Flight International. Our work was often with Indigenous people, and I am grateful for all of the wisdom imparted to me from within these Indigenous communities. It was in these groups that I began to learn about the first-hand experience and the intergenerational impact of Residential Schools. I recall one man telling me that he was taken from his family at the age of three. I think of my granddaughter, who is now just three years old, and my heart breaks for this little boy. He was just a baby. After being taken from their homes and separated from their parents, many children in Residential Schools experienced mental, emotional, physical, sexual, and spiritual abuse, all traumatic experiences. I am grateful to Dr. Simington for the knowledge, wisdom, and experience that she shared with me and with her other students.

I trained with Dr. Simington and then worked alongside her using, amongst other modalities, deep meditation or trance work, spirituality, ritual and ceremony, creativity, cognitive behavioural strategies, and psychoeducation to help people heal from trauma. Dr. Simington has written two books, *Journey to the Sacred: Mending the Fractured Soul*, and *Setting the Captive Free.* I urge you to check them out if you are looking for resources to learn about and heal from trauma and grief, or if you are simply interested in exploring your own spirituality. You may also wish to check out her website, www.takingflightinternational.com. It was during this time of learning with Dr. Simington that I began my ongoing love affair with the amazing brain we each have.

While working towards my Master's Degree, I had the privilege of working at Poundmaker's Addiction Treatment Centre in St. Albert, Alberta, and also the Men's Spiritual Healing Lodge in Prince Albert, Saskatchewan. I learned extensively about trauma from both experiences. While at Poundmaker's Lodge, I encountered the impact of trauma on a daily basis when the clients would share their stories. Most of the people being treated for addictions had, at one time or another, been exposed to traumatic events or difficult life experiences. The clients I worked with were, for the most part, using alcohol, drugs, gambling, sex, and other substances to try to soothe themselves. Part of this soothing effort was, no doubt, a learned behavior. At the time I had not yet been exposed to trauma of this magnitude and it was difficult for me to accept that I could not *fix* the people I worked with and cared about. That was not my job. Furthermore, it was not possible.

I PAINT DEAD PEOPLE.

In an effort to cope with my overwhelming feelings of compassion and a sense of powerlessness, I turned to painting, often painting late into the night, even though I am definitely not an artist! At some point I realized that I was painting faces, and more faces, until my living room was full of them. I remember standing at my easel one night, well past midnight, when the words "I paint dead people," came out of my mouth. The hair on the back of my neck stood up, and that is when I realized that painting these faces helped me to understand that my job was not to fix people, but rather to be a witness to their experience and their pain, and to pass along whatever tools I could so that they might do the work themselves. It seemed that I was painting the people who had never been heard, never been seen. Finally, with this realization, I was able to do my job.

My second practicum was at the Men's Spiritual Healing Lodge, and the men who lived there were, in many ways, also my teachers. The Healing Lodge was a place for Indigenous men from Provincial and Federal prison who were not considered high risk. Their crimes ranged from drunk driving to more serious offenses. Most often the crimes occurred while the men were under the influence of drugs or alcohol. The setting was beautiful, and the woman who had the vision and the wherewithal to make it happen was Norma Green. Norma is a gentle but determined woman, who is filled with compassion but never hoodwinked. I was fairly naïve and benefitted greatly from her experience. Having worked for much of her life in the prison system, Norma has seen and heard more than most of us ever will, and her generosity of spirit is rarely, if ever, taken advantage of. She treated the men with respect and garnered theirs in return. The Lodge was situated in the country, and the men stayed in small cabins. It was peaceful and quiet, the kind of atmosphere that created a sense of family. It was conducive to healing.

When I first interacted with the men I felt that they might be suspicious of me, a white woman barging into their world, knowing nothing about them and their lives. Who was I to tell them how to live? Norma calmed my fears and told me to give them a chance to get to know me. Much to their credit, the men were kind to me, and welcomed me into their midst. They treated me with a gentle respect. I was very aware of my white privilege and worried that I might offend them. To break the ice, I told them a story about a crow trying to fly with the eagles and how that crow really didn't have a clue how to do that; and then I admitted that I was for certain feeling very much like that crow. We all had a good laugh, and that was the beginning of one of the best experiences of my life. It didn't take long for me to realize that for many of them, trauma was front and centre in their childhoods. For many, their current situation was directly related to intergenerational violence and/or substance abuse, often associated with the aftermath of the Residential School system.

The men were not big talkers in a group, but when we would meet one on one, they were comfortable telling me their stories. I was touched by the fact that they trusted me to the extent that they did. I learned about their sadness and their regret for the things that they had done, and how they longed for peace and forgiveness. I heard about the difficult and traumatic circumstances in their lives and the many losses they had experienced. I heard over and over again about how powerless they felt when they watched disrespect and violence being perpetrated against their mothers, and they were too little to do anything about it. Mostly I learned about how they yearned for healing.

One day I decided that I would introduce some art work to the men. The results were astounding. Many of the men believed that they had no talent and were thrilled to discover that they did. It was really wonderful to see many of them feeling pride and excitement about their abilities and accomplishments. Artistic expression (mostly painting and carving) was a way for the men to communicate and a way to redeem some measure of self-esteem. I appreciated the way Norma wholeheartedly supported the men in their endeavours.

I remember many of the men vividly, even though this was many years ago. One man in particular looms large in my memory, mostly because I was having great difficulty connecting with him. He would either avoid me or challenge me at every opportunity. I couldn't shake the sense that he was watching me and really didn't like me. I had pretty much given up the idea that he and I would ever connect, until one day he popped into my little office to allegedly talk with me about his upcoming release and finding a job. Since that was neither my area of expertise nor my responsibility, I wasn't sure how I might be able to help him, but I was eager to give it my best shot. We talked…and talked…and talked. I wasn't sure where our conversation was headed, until he said to me, out of the blue, "I want what you've got."

Yes, he certainly had been watching me, and he was able to express to me that what I *had* was a sense of joy and optimism, and he wanted that too. We had the most amazing conversation, one that was the beginning of a brief but meaningful connection. He was released a short time later and I have often wondered, over the years, if he found his joy. I truly do hope so.

What I learned from both of these work experiences was that trauma impacts us in so many negative ways, and until healing happens, it will continue to do so. The effects of trauma can be far-reaching, either within our own lives or intergenerationally. Although this might seem to be overwhelmingly negative, remember this: just as trauma is far-reaching, so too will be the healing. When one person in your family or group begins to heal, others will see this and feel this, and they can't help but be impacted in a positive way. They may even want what you've got.

Trauma is very complex, and we will only scratch the surface here. It is my hope to give you a few basics, and then I urge you to explore and learn more through other resources. I would strongly encourage you to find a therapist who works with trauma, one who will help you begin to unravel the threads of your own experience, which will indeed be unique, while sharing common threads with others.

After the Traumatic Event

The symptoms that present after a traumatic experience are many and varied, and as I stated, unique to each person. You may experience feelings that are unpredictable and overwhelming. You may feel shaken, fearful, anxious, irritable, easily startled, or have mood swings. Your body may experience headaches, muscle tension, nausea, gastrointestinal problems, or fatigue. Yes, the aftermath of trauma can take up residence in your body.

The word nausea often pops up when we talk about anxiety and here is why: we have rich nerve fiber connections between our brain and our gut. When we feel threatened, our brain signals our stomach to secrete more acid and reduce blood flow to the lining, allowing an intense emotion such as anxiety to be felt in our gut. We may experience a drop in our blood levels of the hormone somatostatin, setting ourselves up for gastrointestinal issues. According to Mona Lisa Schulz, M.D., PhD, author of *Awakening Intuition*, chronic anxiety and worry are closely associated with ulcers (a bacterial infection aggravated by stress), as is perfectionism.

Experiencing a trauma can also cause unpleasant images to intrude upon your thinking, or you might have flashbacks (flashing back to the event as if it were real); you may sweat a lot or have an increased heart rate. It might become difficult for you to concentrate or make decisions. You could find that you become disoriented easily. Sleeping and eating patterns may become disrupted.

Many use alcohol, drugs, or some other substance in an attempt to soothe themselves. Some may isolate themselves, becoming withdrawn, avoiding people in general. Others shut down emotionally, often saying no when family or friends extend an invitation to participate in gatherings. Still others may become aggressive, angry, depressed, or numb.

There are many more ways that trauma can affect you, physically, mentally, emotionally, and spiritually. The good thing is that there are strategies that you can use to help yourself. I would again encourage you to get yourself to a therapist who knows how to work with trauma, or perhaps find a group of trauma survivors who meet under the direction of a qualified leader. Having the opportunity to share your story, to be heard, can be invaluable. Then, after being heard and affirmed, learning some strategies to cope will be essential to your recovery. There are some excellent therapists out there who can help you.

I recently watched a remarkable documentary on the POV series on PBS television, by Argot Pictures, called *Almost Sunrise*. It was the story of two US Iraq veterans, Tom Voss and Anthony Anderson, who were suffering from post-war trauma. They decided to embark on a 2,700-mile trek across America, from Wisconsin to California, to try to put their trauma behind them. For the first time, I heard an important discussion about the issue of *moral pain* that some soldiers experience when they return from war. This pain stems from the nagging feeling that some soldiers have that perhaps they have done something wrong. It is a raw, primitive feeling of guilt.

These soldiers have done exactly what they were supposed to do — "fight for our freedom." They train hard, they come to a land not their own, and while striving to do good, they perhaps inflict harm or even kill. They witness horrendous things being done to their fellow soldiers and also to the civilians they are trying to help. They may be physically injured themselves. Then they return home to a society where this behaviour would be punished if it were committed outside of war. They begin to wonder why they were sent to do what they did.

All too often, in hindsight, they learn that the war was never about protecting freedom. Soldiers begin to question whether or not they can be forgiven, whether or not they can forgive themselves, and sometimes whether or not they can forgive their politicians and their God for letting it all happen. The documentary showed how these men, through their walk, their encounters with others, ceremony, and group work began to heal from their trauma, and how they have taken that healing forward to help other veterans. The documentary was deeply touching and dealt with some important issues. I recommend it highly.

I am compelled to say that I am proud of our Canadian soldiers who embark on peace-keeping missions around the world, prepared also to defend our freedom if necessary. We clearly need to do much more for our soldiers when they return home. Peace keepers can and do experience Post Traumatic Stress Disorder, or as it is also commonly known, PTSD, addictions, anxiety, depression, homelessness, family break-down, and other mental health issues. Our soldiers struggle to normalize traumatizing experiences that are simply not normal and often incomprehensible. Lt. Gen. Romeo Dalllaire's life, and his book, *Shake Hands with The Devil,* have had a profound and lasting effect on me. I encourage you to read his book.

Current Treatments and Research

There is much research being done to increase our knowledge about trauma and how we treat it, particularly in light of the difficulties being experienced by returning soldiers. I wish to share some of this information with you, but first, I'm going to provide you with some information about trauma that may surprise you.

- Despite the fact that research and treatment funds are often geared to responding to the needs of the military, there are more civilians than soldiers who experience trauma, and more women than men. Sadly, one factor in the greater incidence of PTSD among women is sexual assault.
- One type of trauma discussed less often is vicarious trauma (the transference of trauma from the actual victim

to another) and it can happen, for example, between parent and child, between one peer to another, or between trauma worker and client.

- Repeated exposure to traumatic events contributes signifi-cantly to the incidence of Post Traumatic Stress Disorder, often occurring amongst first responders, police officers, and other professionals (and I would include counsellors in that list). We therapists are aware that we need to debrief and seek help when we are exposed over and over again to trauma. We are mindful of and vigilant about the importance of not taking on our client's trauma.

- Factors that may make you more vulnerable to PTSD include childhood trauma, pre-existing anxiety and depres-sion, and a lack of a good support system.

Currently the treatment of PTSD involves psychotherapy, includ-ing cognitive behavioural therapy, as well as prolonged exposure therapy, and group therapy. Animals such as dogs and horses are also used in trauma treatment. Some clinicians use tapping (Thought Field Therapy) which is based on principals of contemporary clini-cal psychology and Chinese medicine to tap the body's energy and clear up blockages. If you are interested in learning more about tapping, you may wish to check out a book by Roger J. Callahan, PhD, with Richard Trubo, called *Tapping the Healer Within.*

Other clinicians use EMDR – Eye Movement Desensitization and Reprocessing. Simply put, EMDR is a procedure where the client makes eye movements while thinking about the traumatic event. Many counsellors use this modality and have found success. Because each client is unique, so too are the results of using EMDR. I know of one counsellor who has used a combination of EMDR and Art Therapy and she has sometimes had some remark-able results. I have not used EMDR with my clients. It takes special training, and my work has taken me in other directions. But I have experienced this modality as a client while being counselled.

My personal experience with EMDR involved me talking about my traumatic situation while looking at a long bar of lights that flashed spontaneously in no particular order. I cannot divulge the circumstances of my situation here because they involve another person who is entitled to privacy; I can say, however, that I was unable to get over the traumatic nature of my experience and it involved me crying all the time – hardly conducive to being able to go to work or function in the world. I saw a counsellor who recommended, after a couple of sessions, that we give EMDR a try. It took only one session for me to achieve success. I told my story while watching these lights flashing on and off, while the counsellor asked me guiding questions. During that experience, I was able to come to an understanding of why the situation was so traumatizing for me, and with that understanding, I found clarity and peace.

I also saw remarkable results in Dr. Jane Simington's work involving deep trance, along with several other healing modalities. As suggested previously, you may wish to check out her books and her website. Researchers continue to explore new ways to understand and treat trauma. I recently watched an excellent program on CBC Television, Dr. David Suzuki's *The Nature of Things*, entitled *Beyond Trauma*. I learned that research is being done to determine why it is that people can experience similar events but may have very different PTSD symptoms.

Dr. Ruth A. Lanius is conducting research at Western University in London, Ontario. She has observed that the brain scans of individuals who have experienced the same event can be markedly different. She worked with one couple who were in the same accident but had quite different types of PTSD; one of them experienced emotional shutdown while the other experienced increased, intense emotional activity. The brain scans confirmed their different reactions to the trauma.

Beyond Trauma also highlighted the work of Dr. Margot Taylor and Dr. Ben Dunkley at the Toronto Hospital for Sick Children. They have been doing research to try to find out why some people are more susceptible to PTSD than others. Two people may experience similar events but only one of them has PTSD. They have tracked brain activity and observed consistent patterns of over-active communication between key areas of the brain in people who have PTSD. It has been determined that in soldiers with PTSD, communication between the memory and the emotion areas of the brain is much more active. Not surprisingly, these soldiers feel relief when they are able to see their own brain scans. This is very empowering for them. Their invisible injury becomes tangible and real, not just to them, but to others as well. They can then begin to heal.

I also learned that work is currently being done at the Massachusetts General Hospital in Boston to create a brain implant to be used when all other options fail. The premise is that the brain is an electrical organ and when someone has PTSD, it is because there has been electrical interference. They then attempt to stimulate the brain to bring it back to its original state. Electrodes are guided to spots in the brain where abnormal electrical signals have been detected. During surgery the electrical signals are carefully tuned until symptoms subside. It is complicated work. First, they must isolate the areas of the brain affected, then determine what type of stimulation is required and where it should go, and finally, they must create an implant that is small enough to fit into the brain, where it will remain to continue the stimulation. Much more neuroscientific research is needed to make this treatment viable.

Dr. Alain Brunet at Montreal's McGill University is proposing a cheaper, faster treatment that involves the use of beta-blocking drugs (currently used to stimulate receptors responsible for increased cardiac action that help control heart rhythm, treat angina, and reduce blood pressure). He has been using these drugs to reduce his patients emotional response to fearful memories for the past ten years and has achieved some measure of success. He gives his patients the beta-blocking drug and then has them write the story of their traumatic experience. Once the account is written, he then has the patient read this account aloud. One week later, they come back to his office and read the same account. Improvement is reported in many cases after three or four treatments, and in some cases six treatments.

I discovered, while listening to the CBS evening news on September 18, 2018, that there is important research being done into MDMA-assisted psychotherapy. The CBS reporter interviewed a man by the name of John, who suffered from a traumatic brain injury and severe PTSD as a result of his work as a sniper during the Iraq War. After numerous suicide attempts and other failed therapies, he agreed to try MDMA-assisted psychotherapy. He experienced 3 sessions of 6 to 8 hours with a psychotherapist, while under the influence of MDMA. I understand that this is often accompanied by a further 12 psychotherapeutic sessions without the drug, allowing treatment to be completed in about 4 months.

Basically, what the MDMA does is reduce the activity in the amygdala (the fear processing part of the brain), allowing for the fearful emotions linked to the trauma to be more easily recalled and processed. Only 24 vets were tested, but according to the CBS news report an astounding 68% reported that they completely eliminated their PTSD symptoms and the remaining 32% reported that they significantly reduced their symptoms – and that this didn't change one-year post treatment! The subject named John said, during his interview, that his suicidal thoughts were completely gone, and that he was feeling "normal" again.

You might just be inspired to do some further research on your own. A word of caution: using this drug as a party drug will not help you with your PTSD. It is thought that perhaps one of the important factors in the success of this therapy is that a very close bond is formed between the PTSD client and a qualified therapist who is able to work with PTSD.

I will not dwell further on the specific professional treatments available but urge you to discover and learn more on your own. I would now like to give you some suggestions as to how you might help yourself before you access professional treatment, during treatment, and following treatment. In fact, these ideas can be used for a lifetime by all of us.

How to Take Care of Yourself Post Trauma

Post Traumatic Stress Disorder is often invisible, but just as we care for the gash on our leg, so too must we care for ourselves after a traumatic experience. How do we do this self-care? One thing you can do immediately is to use calming self-talk. Remember when I told the stories – story one and story two – of my experience of preparing to drive in a blizzard? I can talk myself up (increase my anxiety) or talk myself down (decrease my anxiety). It's my choice. While doing this self-talk, it's important to minimize your negative thoughts. Pay attention to the language you use, both externally and internally. When you are feeling unsafe, it is easy to ramp up the negative thoughts – much easier than creating the calming thoughts. But it can be done.

It is important to do a reality check, every single time your anxiety ramps up. The most important question to ask yourself is this: "Am I in danger?" Then take the time to observe your surroundings, and note specifically that there is nothing in your environment that is dangerous. Tell your brain, out loud, "We (you and your brain) are not in danger here. We are okay."

After trauma, self-care is ongoing, building positively from one day to the next. For this reason, it is important to create and maintain balance in your life – to care for yourself mentally, emotionally, physically, and spiritually. We will talk later about that in more depth, but suffice it to say that the areas noted below are key. I urge you to promote balance and health in all four areas, whether you have experienced trauma or not. All four areas are important for your overall health.

Physical

- Eat healthy, nutritious food on a regular basis throughout the day.
- Have adequate rest and sleep – as much as you possibly can. Even if you can't sleep, rest can be helpful. Be aware of sleeping too much (more than 8 hours a day).
- Maintain a daily exercise regimen (something that you find fun and invigorating).
- Limit or eliminate alcohol and drugs (including caffeine).
- Attend to cleanliness and appearance. If you normally get your hair done, or have a pedicure or manicure, keep it up.
- Consider having massages, even if this is not your norm. Explain to your massage therapist that you have experienced a recent trauma and that you are on edge.
- Be sure to take prescribed medications when required.
- Do daily breath work. Nice deep breaths in to the count of five, out to the count of six, thinking "slow" on the in-breath and "down" on the out-breath.
- Most importantly, listen to your body. Do what it needs you to do.

Mental

- Pay attention to how you are using your brain. Often when we find it difficult to concentrate, learning something new can distract and entertain us, especially if we are really interested in it.

- Monitor your self-talk, keeping negative thoughts to a minimum.

- Be creative. Expressing your feelings about the trauma through a creative medium is seriously beneficial. Painting, singing, dancing, gardening, writing, cooking, sewing and quilting, building – whatever you love to do, do it. You may not feel like getting started, but get started, and the comfort will follow.

- Resume your normal activities as soon as possible. Sitting home alone, dwelling on what happened – well, you know where that will lead – to one negative thought after another.

- Begin to learn other strategies to reduce stress and anxiety.

Emotional

- Prioritize your safety and health needs. Make a point of ensuring your own safety.

- Have the quiet time that you need.

- Seek the support of others who care about you. Tell them what you need from them. If all you need right then is for them to listen, tell them that.

- Seek support from others who have experienced a trauma similar to yours. Group support, led by a qualified leader, can be invaluable. Note: If you find that the support group you join is negative, non-productive, and full of complainers, stop going. Find a new group.

- Communicate your experience in whatever way feels helpful *to you.* Say as much or as little as you want to say.

Remember, this is your experience, these are your feelings. There is no right way to feel, and no wrong way to feel. What you feel is what you feel.

- Know that you will be grieving what happened to you, and that it takes time for grief and anxiety to lessen. Know that it will take time for you to once again regulate and manage your reactions. But also know that *you can do it!*

- Talk with a therapist or medical specialist, and get the help you need. Try to find someone who works with trauma, and if that person is not available to you, find someone who works with anxiety.

- Use the support that is offered to you, but be discerning. If something is helpful to you, continue with it. If it is not helpful to you, stop using it.

- Pay attention to your own resilience. We all have resilience, to some degree or another. Celebrate each step of your progress. Remember, your brain needs to hear that you are the one in charge; you are the boss of you, and you will take care of you.

Spiritual

- Think about what spiritual means to you. Embrace what it offers.

- If you are religious and belong to a religious community, whether it be Muslim, Christian, Hindu, Buddhist, or some other religion, reach out as much as you are comfortable. Sing, drum, pray, meditate, congregate.

- If spirituality for you is about meaning and purpose, rethink your life in terms of meaning and purpose. Moving forward, how will you find meaning? Will your purpose remain the same? What things offer you joy and contentment and give you a sense of satisfaction?

- If spirituality means connection to the earth, to others, to yourself, you may wish to spend some time in nature, (very healing!) spend time with others who 'get you,' or spend time in solitude (but watch that you are not isolating yourself too much).

- This bears repeating – spend time in nature. Climb a mountain, go on a hike, go to the beach, lay in a farmer's field, garden in your back yard, walk in the rain, read a book in the sun – all of these things will help to heal your pain.

- If your culture is important to you, connect with others who celebrate your culture; if you have lost your culture, connect with others who can teach you; enjoy traditions within your own home. If you don't have any, create some.

- Once again, I must mention gratitude. You are creating a new way for your brain to interpret the world. Doing your daily gratitudes is really essential to your spiritual and emotional well being. Take the time to express gratitude.

I have discovered over the years that I am a spiritual optimist. This notion began to dawn on me after my series of seven dreams, where I was told over and over again that everything is under control – just not under my control. Perhaps what ultimately makes me a spiritual optimist is that I believe that each wound we suffer and eventually heal from is an important part of our evolving, growing, learning self. As we grow and learn and make our way toward wholeness, many of us begin to realize that our own personal learning is a part of the healing of humanity.

I have watched a spiritual optimism unfold over the past several months in the midst of hurricane and fire disasters, volcano eruptions, and gun violence resulting in untold injury and death. I've heard stories of kindness, inclusiveness, courage, and coming together. I know, as I write this, that there are some dark days ahead for some of us, but it is my hope that as human beings, we will always come together to care for each other with compassion.

Mind-Body Connection

Keep in mind the importance of mind-body connection when dealing with trauma. A cognitive approach to trauma treatment is important, but increasingly, we find that the experts are taking into consideration the idea that our body must also be a part of this treatment.

Our minds can be slippery, and because we have worked long and hard to put our defenses in place, to build our walls, it might take a long time to penetrate these walls. This is where our bodies become our mind's helpers. Our bodies have no time or patience for emotional walls. If we are touched physically in the right way, these walls can simply fall away. I do know from experience that any time I have had a treatment such as Body Talk, or have practiced yoga consistently, I have learned a great deal from my body about my emotions, sometimes hidden from my consciousness. When I practice yoga on a regular basis, my stress levels automatically decline. It is interesting that social neuroscience research now shows evidence to support the theory that if you calm your body, you will calm your mind.

It is important to breathe properly, because our breathing can be a powerful tool when it comes to affect regulation – changing how you feel in your body. Trauma survivors often breathe in a rapid, shallow manner. If you think about shallow breathing, it often happens when we are in a state of hyper-arousal, anxiety, or panic. I don't know about you, but when I am frightened, I sometimes hold my breath too. This is another kind of defense mechanism and can be used as a protection against overwhelming emotion, but it can leave us feeling agitated and anxious. Completing some nice, slow belly breaths can help us release some of that agitation and anxiety.

Again, I stress the importance of a balanced approach. We are not one-dimensional human beings. We are complex creatures who benefit from a multi-dimensional approach to working with our anxiety. Think about how you care for yourself in each of these areas, and how you might add to that in a meaningful way. We will do an exercise later to help you use this practice of balance as a part of your daily living.

If you have anxiety as a result of a traumatic situation, I urge you to see a therapist who can help you with the anxiety and potential post traumatic stress that can result from your experience. There is help out there.

Using Ritual and Ceremony to Heal

We incorporate many rituals into the fabric of our lives – marriage, baptism, graduations, communion in church, and funerals are just some examples. Rituals are taught to us, and they can also be something we create for ourselves. I recall taking a class called *The Spiritual Practice of Drawing the Mandala.* At the outset, we were each asked to do a morning ceremony, to help us understand the benefits of ceremony. Since I can't draw a stick figure, I was a little worried about drawing a mandala. I decided to create a *Dear Art* ritual.

I wrote a letter to Art (much like a Dear John letter) where I was basically breaking up with Art. I had been highly self-critical of my artistic abilities my entire life, and I wanted that to stop. I had not talked kindly to Art, to put it mildly! I drew a picture of the Art Monster, and when it was my turn to lead the ceremony, I invited the twelve women in my class to join me in a circle on the floor, with a candle in the middle. I read my Dear Art letter, apologizing to Art for all the mean things I had said to him and about him, and asked him to consider having a new, healthy relationship with me. I then showed the women my really abysmal sketch of the Art Monster and told the women that if they would like to end their dysfunctional relationship with Art, they could join me in tearing off a piece of the Art Monster and burning it in the fire. Much to my surprise, every single woman joined in. After the burning of the Art Monster, I felt really excited to tackle the class, having created the beginnings of a new relationship with Art. I thoroughly enjoyed the class; I also reaffirmed that I will never be a talented artist and I am totally okay with that!

I discovered the importance of ritual and ceremony for healing purposes during my work with Indigenous people at Poundmaker's Lodge and then again at the Men's Spiritual Healing Lodge. My experience using these modalities was affirmed and augmented when I studied and then worked with Dr. Simington at Taking Flight International. Ritual can be very helpful when dealing with the aftermath of one traumatic experience or many. You can create rituals to use for yourself. You can do them by yourself or with others. Rituals are sacred expressions of our need to heal.

At Poundmaker's Lodge, clients attended a six-week residential program. Our day was scheduled with group work, private counselling sessions, education, creative work, chores, fun gatherings, and so on. Our mornings would begin with a staff meeting where we would smudge together (using sacred smoke to cleanse and purify) and say the Serenity Prayer together.

"God, grant me the serenity to accept the things I cannot change, the courage to change the things I can, and the wisdom to know the difference." Niebuhr.

I had no idea initially how important that ritual would become for me as I navigated unfamiliar waters.

At the end of each six-week period, we would have a graduation ceremony (another ritual). As each person went up to speak and receive their graduation certificate, it never ceased to amaze me how differently the clients presented themselves in comparison to their first day. When I first met them, their heads were down, faces often obscured by greasy or dry, lifeless hair, shoulders sagging and slumped. On graduation day the situation was much different. Women pulled their hair back so that we could see their bright, eager faces. They smiled and looked everyone in the eye. They spoke with confidence and pride. Men shaved, spruced up their hair, carried themselves with dignity, and they smiled too. Everyone was smiling. Perhaps for many it was the first time in their lives that they were able to stand so proudly.

At the Men's Spiritual Healing Lodge, sweats (sacred purifying rituals) and feasts were important. For the men it was a time of bonding and celebration, a time to cleanse, to understand their anger, to share their grief, and to seek forgiveness. When it was time for me to leave the Lodge, I was deeply honoured when the men invited me to a sweat. They made a goodbye for me. I will never forget the sacredness of the ritual we experienced together and the joy I felt sharing this moment with them.

I recall another sweat that I attended with Norma Green that was just for women. It took place outside of the Healing Lodge and was a special celebration for a young woman who was coming of age. How wonderful for this young woman to be lifted up in such an important way!

This sweat was a time for friends, family, and community to come together to celebrate, share, and connect. It was a sacred time of honouring. Most importantly, it was a time for this young woman to learn how beautiful it is to be a woman and how she is deserving of respect and dignity. After the sweat we attended a feast, and the best part was when we women sat in a circle eating, talking, and laughing...while the men served us. It was their way of honouring the women who gathered together. What could be better?

Ritual and ceremony are about connecting with and honouring the sacred within ourselves. That is healing work. As you move towards the healing of your own trauma, you may wish to consider adding some ritual or ceremony to the work you are doing. The benefits are immediate and they are profound.

CHAPTER FOURTEEN
Anxiety in a Social Setting

For some, being in a classroom, a meeting, a workplace setting, or a social gathering can be excruciating; however, social connection is a basic feature of our human experience, and when we are deprived of that connection, we suffer. Mlodinow discusses, in *Subliminal*, the research into how social pain is associated with a part of the brain structure called the anterior cingulate cortex – the same structure involved in the emotional component of physical pain – just another study confirming that our minds and our bodies are beautifully connected and interwoven, for our benefit. This affirms what I have long known – we must involve our bodies in the treatment of the anxiety we are feeling.

Let's have a look now at what social anxiety is, how it might manifest, and what we might do about it. I mentioned my client Billy previously and recounted some of the physical symptoms and head chatter that he experienced when faced with a social setting. I will again talk about some of those symptoms, because you may find that you recognize yourself in this type of situation.

First, we'll talk about the head chatter. It goes like this:

- "I'm such a dork. They all think I'm stupid."
- "I'm sweating through my shirt, and my hands are wet. They can all see it. I'm totally a Stink Guy."

- "Oh God, oh God, oh God, get me out of here. Please, God, let me sink through the floor."
- "These women think they are really hot stuff. I can't get out of here fast enough."
- "Do NOT come over here and speak to me!"
- "That's it. I'm never coming here again."

Along with the head chatter, we have the body alarms going off.

- Pounding heart (or irregular rhythm)
- Profuse sweating
- Fast, shallow breathing (from chest)
- Dry mouth
- Shaking hands
- Tingling in arms, legs, mouth
- Headache
- Deer in the headlights or angry, scowling facial expressions
- Nausea
- Sharp pains in abdomen
- Tight face, neck, shoulders, back
- Clenched teeth…or fists

No doubt there are many more. Remember, we are each unique, and we each experience anxiety in a unique way.

The anxiety we feel is not merely about the one hour that we're present in the dreaded situation. Oh no, it's much bigger than that. We must not forget *anticipatory anxiety!* How much time and energy do you spend dreading an event that is to take place a week from now? How much time do you spend dreading an event that may never take place? How much time do you spend listing all the things that might go wrong in a social encounter this afternoon, or tomorrow, or next year? I'll wager a great deal of time is spent in anticipatory anxiety mode. I'm speaking from experience.

We also have *post event anxiety*, where you constantly turn over and over again in your mind how things went, how they should have gone, what you did wrong, why it was a complete and total catastrophe, what a dork you are, and how you never, ever want to do that again. In both cases, you have increased your anxiety exponentially and certainly set yourself up for even greater anxiety the next time. The reality is, most people who have anxiety have the capacity to be super self-critical. The ways you might find to criticize and lash out at yourself are almost limitless. You're probably quite good at that. Sadly, it may be one of your best skills.

Why are we not kinder to ourselves? Everything I've written does not apply to social anxiety only. It applies to *all* anxiety! What if you were to create a life where you, too, are deserving of blessings and love and compassion? What might happen if you decided to stop judging yourself in such a harsh manner, and instead began to accept that you are a truly mortal being who is on this earth to learn, love, and be? What if you were to begin to love yourself as much as you love the people who are most precious to you?

Why not take one step? It will be okay.

Let's have a look at how you might begin to prepare yourself for social connection.

Framework to Practice Social Anxiety Strategies

Sometimes, putting ourselves in the most comfortable position possible is a great way to start. Certainly, choosing familiar territory and areas of high interest would be beneficial and a good place to initially practice strategies before branching out into less familiar territory. Are you used to the crowd at your aunt Linda's house? Excellent! A good place to start. Do you love star gazing more than anything in the world? Another good place to start, but only if you go to a conservatory with other like-minded star-gazers, rather than looking at the stars all by yourself in your own back yard.

Once you have your favourite strategies down pat, (and it will take some practice) it will be time to branch out to situations where you are a little less familiar with the people or the events going on. Use the same strategies – you will most likely find that they work for you in exactly the same way. It may take a bit of time to reach a level of comfort, but that is okay – every step forward counts! The best part is that you'll feel better and better with each step.

The final step on your road to success will be to branch out to completely new situations. Again, use the same strategies that have worked for you in the first two situations. But remember – one step at a time. And while you're remembering that, you can also remind yourself that *movement creates movement.* You'll accomplish nothing if you stay home and read a book or watch TV. This will require practice, and this is a good time to call on the people who care about you to help you practice.

Social anxiety is not a personal failure and should not be embarrassing. It has to do with the way your brain functions. My brain decided, when I was young, that I was going to be lousy at math. I often needed help and learned to ask for it. If I hadn't received the help, I might have failed every math exam. When I asked for and received the necessary assistance, I succeeded, by the skin of my teeth. But the important point is…I succeeded.

One really great way to practice your strategies for socializing with strangers is by doing volunteer work. This is usually a comfortable setting, because you and the other volunteers are doing the same type of work, giving you something to talk about right away. You'll be new to the situation – a great opportunity to ask questions and become familiar with the task you will be doing, a great reason to interact. You'll soon be experiencing a sense of accomplishment together, which will no doubt offer you, and the person working next to you, the opportunity for more communication. You'll have the added bonus of meeting someone who shares your interests – after all, you have both chosen the same type of experience.

If you're at an animal shelter, it's likely safe to assume that you and the person you're working alongside both enjoy being with animals. If you're volunteering at a homeless shelter, you're both likely compassionate people, caring about those who are less fortunate than you are. If you're volunteering with a youth group, you likely share an appreciation for young people. If you find yourself coaching sports, you most likely both enjoy sports and working with people. I think you get my drift by now.

Identifying Your Unique Strengths and Challenges

Let's do an exercise to help you identify where you feel most confident and least confident. Grab a pen and notebook and start writing.

1. List your symptoms of social anxiety, making sure that you include symptoms for how your thoughts, feelings, and behaviour are affected. Be specific. Really listen to your internal dialogue, listing the positive thoughts and the negative thoughts. Do the same with your feelings and your behaviors.

2. Notice what you feel in your body – be specific – where is that feeling, what is that feeling? This awareness will help you to become more attuned to the specific challenges you are facing. After all, you can't change what you can't identify, right?

3. Outline what you want to be different, in terms of each symptom. Be specific. This will help you to visualize the outcome you want.

4. Name the strengths that you have that will help you to make specific changes to all of the things that you've listed. Don't be hard on yourself – you DO have strengths! I suggest that you ask your friends and family to help you with this list.

5. Determine whether you are an extrovert or an introvert, as you will likely socialize differently depending on which you are. We tend to focus on extroverts in our society, and extroverts tend to have an easier time when it comes to socializing. If you are an introvert, learn everything you can about what feels most comfortable for an introvert such as yourself, and socialize in the way that fits you best. For example, if one-on-one socializing feels best to you, seek out that type of encounter. Even when you're in a larger group, you can connect with one person at a time. If you aren't an introvert, take time to get to know one. I have a few introverts in my life, and I value them highly.

As an introvert, (apparently one third of us are) you may have many people in your life who don't understand you. You may even have trouble understanding yourself occasionally. I married an introvert, and my daughter is an introvert, and it took me 20 years to begin to understand even a little bit about what life is like for an introvert. One resource I found to be helpful is Susan Cain's book, *Quiet: The Power of Introverts in a World That Can't Stop Talking.* You may wish to check it out.

6. Enlist your helper to practice with you. Set aside a couple of hours every week to practice specific strategies.

7. Continue to work on these strategies until you feel ready to put yourself in a social situation. Use the strategies that work for you. Discard the strategies that don't work for you.

8. Don't try to be someone you're not. You are loveable exactly as you are!

What Are Some Basic Strategies?

- **Smile!** Smiling is a wickedly good tool to use! Here is why: smiling releases neuropeptides that help fight stress, as well as endorphins that are natural pain relievers. Smiling also releases serotonin, which acts as an anti-depressant, and dopamine, which signals pleasure. What a gift! Smiling will simply make you feel better, and it will also relax the person you wish to engage with. The person on the receiving end of your smile will likely smile back at you, thus getting all the benefits of that smile. You will both be off to a good start.

- Speaking of dopamine, do what you can to activate dopamine in healthy ways, such as playing, laughing, expressing gratitude and kindness, complimenting someone, and exercising. You will feel the pleasure response, and it will help to set you at ease.

- Watch what other people are doing; listen to how they start a conversation. Gather a tip or two, and then search for the person who is standing or sitting alone, not engaged in conversation. Approach them, introduce yourself, and perhaps make a general comment on the event that you're attending (something positive, unless, of course, it's the most disgusting thing you've ever attended).

- Look at people's faces (especially the eyes) when you speak to them. Remember, our eyes are the windows to our soul. Even though eye contact may be difficult for you, it will most likely make the other person feel much more comfortable talking with you.

- **Smile!** You will actually look more attractive to people. If they smile back at you, and they likely will, *they* will also become more attractive to *you*.

- Listen carefully to what the other person says to you. Don't stop listening to them so that you can plan your response to what they're saying, because you'll need to hear everything they say before you can decide how you want to respond.

- Don't mumble. Don't cover your mouth when you speak or laugh. If eyes are the window to the soul, your mouth is the window to your brain. Remember, your brain is awesome. Let it work for you.

- Have a drink – water or whatever suits you – in the event that you have a dry mouth.

- Speaking of drinking...don't get drunk. It won't help you, not in the long run. You might even embarrass yourself – a lot. I'm not necessarily saying I know this from experience, but I am a work in progress.

- **Smile!** I know. I'm repeating this one. It's important. You don't need to plaster a humongous grin on your face. A small smile that touches your lips and your eyes will do nicely.

- Nice deep breaths from the belly. Slow and steady.

- Ask questions. People (maybe not you, but most people) like to talk about themselves. You don't have to be nosey to appear interested. Being interested in someone is complimentary to them. You might ask them if they are enjoying the event. You may want to introduce yourself, tell them what you think about the event, and then ask them if they attend this type of thing often, or if it is their first time. If I were at an art gallery, I might ask someone what they think of a painting. If I'm at an outdoor sporting event, I might ask who they are cheering for. How you approach this will really be dependent on the occasion.

- Admit when you don't know something. Show that you are interested in learning about it by asking questions.

- **Smile!** I'm totally serious about this one, as you have no doubt gathered by now. According to Mlodinow, research shows that we engage the parts of our brain linked to reward processing when we participate in acts of mutual cooperation – another reason to be nice to people, and to engage in volunteer work. The rewards are built in and *will* materialize. Two people sharing a smile is certainly what I would consider to be an *act of mutual cooperation.*

- Ask someone if they would like to help you with a task that will assist you or your host.

- Use non-verbal ways of communicating. Nod your head yes, shake your head no. Show your feelings on your face (surprise, amusement, disgust, puzzlement, compassion, and so on.) Be wary of touching someone you don't know. For some, being touched is very uncomfortable and may provoke a negative response. It can also be misinterpreted as harassment. When it comes to touching, I would suggest that you save that for the people closest to you, who have already signalled that it's okay for you to touch them. On another note, don't be afraid to let someone know that you are not comfortable with touch. It's perfectly okay to say, "Please don't touch me. It makes me feel uncomfortable." No other explanation is needed.

- If you forget someone's name, ask. I forget names all the time. I simply admit that I'm bad at remembering names, apologize, and carry on.

- Introduce people to each other. Be a connector.

- And, of course…

Change is not easy, and sometimes it can feel scary. But on the flip side, the rewards can be enormous. It takes courage to create change, and that change is created when *you are thinking and acting in ways that are new to you.* Fancy that!

Surely, it is time to take a step, one tiny step, to create something new in your own life. Perhaps you will do one interesting thing today that you've never done before, or maybe you'll simply think one new thought today that you didn't think yesterday. Maybe you'll start the practice of gratitude – becoming aware of the things in your life that you are grateful for. You may decide to call a friend you haven't seen in ages and go for coffee, or maybe you'll take a leap and sign up for a painting class, a woodworking class, or even a martial arts class. Any little step will be a good one. I guarantee it.

CHAPTER FIFTEEN

I am the Centre of my Universe... and it's So Painful!

How does this happen, that you become so negatively focused on yourself that you are stumbling and mumbling and cursing yourself sideways and blue? And the more sideways you get, and the bluer things get, the more anxious you feel.

Self-consciousness happens when we focus our attention inward, usually because we believe we will not perform well or believe that we have nothing of value to offer, and we believe that others also believe this about us. In reality, while it's likely true that *you* believe this about yourself, it's just as likely that for others, it will be patently *untrue*. Being focused inward does not solve your problem, but rather makes it worse. It basically means that you don't have enough *attention* to go around. When it's all focused on you, you'll be incapable of paying attention to others, and thus the connection is lost.

To break this self-focus, try to fill your mind with thoughts about the people around you, and thoughts about the event going on around you. You might find yourself thinking about that woman's beautiful hair, or that man's great smile, or that woman's funky dress, or that child's intelligence, or maybe even the beauty of that bird. You may find yourself marvelling at how people, complete strangers, seem to connect with one another. You may choose to focus on the art work on the wall or the marvellous collection of books on the table, which you might even point out to the person sitting next to you!

Don't ever be afraid to compliment other people. To avoid going over the top, you might want to stop short of saying to a stranger, "I'm totally in love with you. You're absolutely freaking beautiful." But there is certainly nothing wrong with saying, "I've been looking forward to talking with you – you have such a great smile." This does not have to be a come on, although I don't mind if you want to try it out.

When you allow yourself to be curious and to ask questions, you encourage the conversation to open up and expand beyond your natural horizons. Others will most likely be eager to engage with you. If they aren't, move on. You may encounter someone who is also socially shy, or awkward, or even anxious. Be kind, smile, and try to set them at ease. Perhaps you might like to share something about yourself with them.

I recall a night in my early University days when I was sitting in the hallway lounge waiting for an evening class to start. Another young woman came and sat down across from me, and simply said, "Hi!" She mentioned that we were in the same class, and we chatted briefly about the class. When we went into the classroom, she sat in front of me, and midway through the class, she turned around and whispered, "Do you drink beer?" I'm happy to say that this was the beginning of a beautiful friendship. It wasn't until many years later that she told me that she was in a dark place that night. She was a reserved young woman but vowed to herself that she would talk to the next person she saw – a sort of last ditch effort. I am deeply grateful that she picked me.

My go-to strategy, the one that helps me to get started in a social situation where I don't know anyone, has always been to look for someone who might be feeling as shy or awkward as I am feeling in that situation, and engage them in conversation. They are usually as grateful as I am to have someone to talk with.

Remember that self-confidence is something that comes and goes. You will have more confidence in some situations than in others. You can often build your own self-confidence by acting as if you are confident. I recall a time in my life when I decided I would simply stop being reticent in social situations. I picked an occasion where not one soul knew me, and I approached it with all the confidence of Meryl Streep. You know what? It worked. People assumed that I was outgoing, gregarious, and utterly social. I even surprised myself! From that day forward, I was able to move more confidently in social settings, simply because I knew I could.

Here is something else you may wish to think about. Do you have people in your life who are always negative? Are they critical of you? This will not help you to change your self-concept. Try to surround yourself with people who have a positive outlook and people who are able to see the goodness in you. They are out there.

Once you have surrounded yourself with positive, uplifting people, pay particular attention to what it is they appreciate about you. Your mind might be thinking, "No way. That's not true," but I challenge you to consider the possibility that it *is* true. I would encourage you to write those positive things down in a journal, and read them over and over again. You may find that the things people see are repetitive, and it might be that in this repetition you begin to see who you really are.

It is often our own fear that holds us back, that makes us want to feel safe at all costs; however, excessive safety behaviours and avoidance will make the problem worse, not better. Have I said this before? Yes, and I will say it again and again. DO NOT LET YOUR FEAR HOLD YOU BACK! YOU CAN DO THIS. Even when it feels risky, try not to protect yourself to the point where you're unable to experience life and feel the joy of connection with others. After all, what do you have to lose? If you take that risk, if you attempt to connect, something *will* change. Take one small step. Movement creates movement!

It is important to understand that we humans are capable of changing not only our thinking *patterns*, but also the specific thoughts we have about ourselves. Research has shown that neuroplasticity absolutely exists in the amygdala, the part of the brain structure that processes emotion and anxiety. This means, in plain and simple terms, change can happen. I'll repeat this important piece of information: when we change how we *think* about ourselves, we will change how we *feel* about ourselves. When we change how we *feel* about ourselves, we will automatically *behave* differently. I can't say it enough...the power of your brain is awesome! What a glorious instrument we have, right in our very own bodies. We don't have to buy a brain, borrow a brain, or beg a brain. We each get one, and we each get to use it to our best advantage. Why not do that?

CHAPTER SIXTEEN
The Dreaded Panic Attack

Panic attacks come and go, usually within five to ten minutes. Ingrained in our psyche is the coming, not so much the going. If you have never had a panic attack, you will not likely understand the intensity of the experience – particularly the physical aspects. These attacks are a bit like anxiety on steroids. Think of the things you feel with everyday anxiety and multiply them by ten. Or fifty. That's a panic attack.

Panic attacks are difficult to forget because of the power of the physical response and the feeling of loss of control. People have mistaken panic attacks for heart attacks or *going crazy*. Panic attacks are neither. Basically, what is happening is that for some reason you have been triggered, and your brain is sending out alarm signals to your body, the old "Danger! Danger! Danger!" Your body is responding appropriately by giving you a rush of adrenalin and cortisol to help you prepare to fight, run away, or freeze on the spot. But remember, this is of steroidal intensity, and your body will go into overdrive to try and help you out. Generally, there is no need for this rush of hormones, because you are not in danger. What it does is make you feel really bad. It's a bit like stepping on the gas when you're up against a brick wall.

Sometimes the attacks are similar to nightmares, in the sense that both are trying to get our attention and give us information. We can get messages in our dreams, but if we don't pay attention to the messages, we may be gifted with a nightmare that will surely get our attention. We also get messages from our body as to the level of stress and anxiety we are feeling. If we don't pay attention to those messages, we may have a panic attack, once again sure to get our attention.

Judy Walker, an old friend of mine, experienced some important and deeply emotional life transitions recently. She felt she was coping reasonably well but was taken by surprise when she had her first panic attack. She wrote about the experience, and I thought she clearly captured the reality of being in the midst of panic, and the utter exhaustion when it was over. She has given me her permission to share her experience with you.

Can You Hear Me Now?

You've been telling me for some time: "Something is off. The instrument is out of tune. Can you not feel it?"

You've asked for my attention and I, like an overwhelmed parent swatting at her child's grubby hand, said:

"Not now!"

"Can't you see I'm busy?"

"I'm fine!"

It goes on like this for weeks. You are patient and I take your silence to mean that you no longer need my attention. I forget I left you in a room with nailed window shutters and locked doors. You are an inconvenience to my busy life, to my to-do-list, my perfectionism, my need to please everyone, see everyone, love everyone… except you.

Yesterday, you pried the shutters open with your bare hands. You screamed so loud the windows shattered. You lunged at the door.

"Get me out of this fucking room," I heard you shout from inside my chest.

I ignore you, shower, pull on my pretty dress, brush eyeshadow on my lids and rouge on my too-pale cheeks, all-the-while shushing you to please stop all that racket. "You are fine," I coo. "We'll walk to work this morning. Won't that be fun?"

"youarefineyouarefinebreathinginbreathingoutyouarefineyouare-fine."

I slow down for a robin. The one serenading on top of the tallest pine tree, a return call coming from across the legislative grounds. "Beautiful song," you say. "Can we stay in a while?"

"We have to go," I say. "There are people depending on me. People inside files, their names in numbered code."

*We make it to 11*th*. Chest tight. Breath shallow.*

"youarefineyouarefineyouarefine."

I exchange pleasantries with the new summer student whose arms are filled with a plant to "brighten" her windowless office.

"youarefineyouarefineyouarefine."

I decide maybe the doctor could help.

"...higher than normal volume of calls," a recorded voice. "Please call again later."

There is no number to press for emergency.

My heart is taking up too much space in my chest, or is it my chest shrinking, shrinking.

"GET HELP!" you shout from somewhere inside me.

I hear you. I hear you.

I shuffle down the hall to a co-worker's office. "I'm not well," I hear someone say and I wonder who's talking?

I can't stop crying. I struggle to catch my breath. My body shakes.

I hate this fuss and drama.

The firemen arrive. "My name is Ben." I watch Ben pull on a blue rubber glove and write down my age and name on the side of his rubbered hand. Ben. I knew a Ben once. He was a good kisser.

The paramedics arrive. There is some back and forth about why Ben didn't give me Aspirin.

"I AM HERE!" I want to shout, but it's not my way.

"Chew these," two Aspirins inside my mouth. "They're orange flavoured."

Ativan under my tongue. "To help you calm down."

I comply.

"Heart rate is fine."

"Blood pressure is a bit low."

"Oxygenation normal."

"…we'll know more once we get you to the hospital for more tests."

In the ambulance. The digital clock above the rear door flashes 9:11. It's not 9:11, this I know because my phone alarm just went off. It's 10:10.

9:11

9:11

9:11

The two paramedics keep bantering about Ben. "I hope he didn't take offence," the one who shoves another Ativan under my tongue says. "I hope he takes it as a learning opportunity."

I feel sorry for young Ben with my age and name on his rubber glove.

Two sprays of nitroglycerin. The chest tightness is now replaced by burning in my solar plexus. (Are you building a bon-fire in there? I'm thinking. Are you?) My hands are buzzing so hard I could probably power the ambulance lights.

"I don't know what's happening to me?" I ask the paramedic who had a thing with Ben.

"It's ok," she says, not looking at me. "You are just scared."

I am so out of it I don't feel a thing.

My co-worker arrives. I'm relieved to see a familiar face. She's kind and tells me about her stay in the very hospital. "It's a good hospital," she says.

My mom arrives. Mark is there. He's wearing my favourite shirt with the blue checkers.

The doctors can't find anything wrong with me. "Oh, the pain in the right breast? Nothing can be done in Emergency for that. See your doctor for a mammogram. It's not something we do in the ER."

In my yellow house. I wonder how I got there? Someone covered me up with a blanket. I'm still wearing the pretty office dress. Am I asleep? I'm so high on Ativan, I have no idea about reality. I think I ask Mark to marry me when I see his kind face leaning over me.

People float around me like cartoon characters. It's just me in my pretty dress and the sun going down behind the shutters. The house is so quiet.

Emma makes me toast with lots of jam and cheddar cheese. "Hey," I say. "It's the same snack your dad made for me after you were born. Remember?"

She doesn't, but she smiles and touches my face.

Sleep comes with her promises of taking it all away.

"Can you hear me now?" You ask one more time.

Panic attacks do not happen in a planned and orderly manner. They do not happen when we are anticipating them. As you can see from Judy's experience, her ability to think through what was happening to her and then make a plan of action to handle that was compromised by the reality of her body being hijacked. She quite simply was not in control of the experience. This is why I suggest that you make a plan in advance if you've had a panic attack and are worried that you might have another one. I would suggest that this plan involve both your thinking and your behavior in order to realize a good outcome.

Five Important Reminders to Use at the Outset

You may recall that we've talked about anxiety in terms of how you think; that you can think your anxiety level up, and you can think your anxiety level down. This is the power that you have, thanks to your *amazing brain*. Some people are able to control the level of their anxiety by reminding themselves that anxiety comes and it goes, and that they have survived it before, and they will again. Both are good thoughts to go through your mind at the outset of the experience.

When you become aware of the sensation of panic it's important that you have your brain on straight, in order to think straight. You're most likely going to feel intense fear at the outset, partly because of the physical symptoms you are experiencing. You will be feeling a perceived loss of control, and also feeling huge anxiety...about the panic attack itself. There are five thought processes that are important to run through your head, to help you get the situation under control. You may wish to write these down on a little card to cue you when you're least likely to *automatically* begin to focus on solutions.

1. Remind yourself that your body is responding to a danger *that does not exist*, and that your body is reacting to help you fight, run away, or freeze, to deal with this imaginary danger.

2. Remind yourself that this is a panic attack (or whatever name you have chosen to call it), and that it is completely harmless. It will not hurt you.

3. Remind yourself that this will last only 5 to 10 minutes, and that you can cope with it because you have learned some powerful strategies to help you. Tell yourself once again that you have survived other similar experiences just fine, and you will survive this one too.

4. Remind yourself again that this is NOT dangerous to you. You will not embarrass yourself. It will pass. Panic comes, panic goes.

5. Remind yourself that anxiety is a thing... It is merely a thing. It is not you. It comes, it goes. It will pass.

Five Ways to Ground Yourself

On the back of this little cue card, you may wish to record the following 5 actions, in abbreviated form, to remind you that you have an active part to play in bringing this situation to a swift resolution.

1. Focus on your breathing. You will likely be shallow-breathing from your upper chest, quite possibly very fast. Or you may hold your breath. It is important to calm your respiratory system, which will in turn help you to calm your whole self, brain included. Begin to do some slow belly breaths, breathing in to the count of 4 and then out to the count of 5. As your breathing begins to slow, you may wish to increase that count to 5 on the in-breath and 6 on the out-breath. Put your hand on your belly button, and make sure that it's moving up and down when you breathe.

    With the in-breath, think the word "slow," and with the out-breath, think the word "down." You're telling your body and your thoughts to *slow…down*. It's helpful to take at least five of these deep breaths, counting down from five to one. For some reason, counting down from 5 rather than counting up from one will help you to focus on the *down* word, the slowing down idea. When you're finished the five breaths, you may wish to take another five if you're not feeling sufficiently calm.

SLOW...DOWN...

2. Ground yourself, using your senses and your environment. Find one thing to look at. Notice the shape, the colour, whether or not it has movement, and so on. Notice one thing

to smell – is it pleasant, strong, weak, or putrid? Notice one thing to touch, and then go and touch it. Is it rough, smooth, wet, or dry? Notice one thing to taste (carry gum or candy in your pocket). Are you tasting something sweet, bitter, sour, or lemony? Notice one thing you can listen to. Is it a voice talking, music, clanking, laughter, or perhaps a whistle? Listen to it and think about what that noise means.

3. Do a reality check. Ask yourself this question: "Am I in danger?" Then take a moment to look around, and notice that there is no danger. Then tell your brain, "Brain, I am not in danger here. There is no need for this over-the-top action. We are safe (you and your brain). We are safe. We are safe." Say all of this out loud, if you're not surrounded by people.

4. You may find it helpful to sing. I got this idea from someone in my family who has experienced panic attacks. She finds that singing helps her enormously. It no doubt helps for several reasons – she loves music, and by singing, she is engaging the creative part of her brain, the area of the brain that processes emotions, and this not only serves as a dis-traction, or re-focus, but it also puts her in her safe place. Singing also helps her to regulate her breath, which in turn helps to regulate her nervous system.

5. Keep doing what you were doing when the panic attack started. Do not run away. Stay in the environment and work your way through it. This will help you to build confidence for the next time it happens. The more confident you become, the less often the panic attacks will come, and the less intense they will be when they do come…and maybe, quite possibly, one day you will no longer have panic attacks!

Another friend and I were recently talking about her anxiety attacks (she chooses this description rather than panic attack). She told me that it is really helpful to her to have a drink of cold water. Another thing she uses when feeling anxious is counting numbers. Counting helps her to regulate herself. Remember, whatever works for you – use it! I do believe that panic attacks can be overcome. It is certainly well worth it to begin to practice the strategies that will help you to do that. Each time you use these strategies, your experience will be less intense and it will happen less often. You *can* take back your life!

There is one more thing I would like you to consider. What if your panic attacks are trying to teach you something, trying, perhaps, to guide you down a new path? Let's use Judy as an example. She worked her way through the anxiety and began to understand that her panic attack was a wake-up call. She has since made changes in her life. She has left a job that provided little opportunity for her to use her considerable creative talents, and has opened herself to the curiosity in her creativity. She was willing to leap, fully acknowledging that the only safety she had was within herself. Judy is now back in school, preparing herself for a new career, and focusing on her writing. She has created a stimulating and thought-provoking blog, *Life Apprentice.* You may wish to check it out at http://lifeapprentice.net – especially if you are all about learning and growing.

PART THREE
Strategies for Moving Forward

CHAPTER SEVENTEEN
Solution Focused Living

I would like to talk a little bit about solution focused living, because anxiety is actually all about *problem focused* living. When we focus on problems, we are more likely to feel helpless and victimized. If we can focus on solutions, we will feel empowered and more in control. How do we do that, exactly?

A few years ago, I was doing some reading about *solution focused* living. At the time, I was the President of a board for an organization that was experiencing some stress. I realized how important it was to focus on solutions rather than problems. I would begin each monthly board meeting with the reminder that we were a solution focused board, and that we would be focusing on solutions in our meeting.

When it came time for the Annual General Meeting, I would start our annual meeting by telling the members at large that we were a solution focused board, and that our meeting would be a solution focused meeting. I assured them that this did not mean that we didn't want to hear their concerns, but rather that I was hopeful that when they stated their concern, they would also suggest a possible solution. The end result was that we always had productive meetings, without repetitive, negative input. The emphasis on being solution focused really did help us to be positive and productive.

This is one of the most important things you will ever teach your children – to be solution focused. They will have significantly less anxiety if they are taught that they are capable of finding a solution to their own problems.

A Framework for Solution Focused Living

Here are some ideas for you, as you begin to set the framework for your very own solution focused life:

- Look for the positive. Try to find even one thing that is positive about your situation.

- Consider that the story can be seen as positive or negative – the glass can be half full or half empty. Remember my driving in the storm stories?

- Remember that you are the expert in your own life. Know that you *will* come up with a positive solution if you focus on solution rather than problem.

- Be aware that you are empowered to handle challenges. You have done it before, and you can do it again.

- Spend time talking about what might work rather than what isn't working. One is productive, the other is not.

- Focus on your strengths and the strengths of others. Focus on and encourage the positive behaviour you want to see, not the negative.

- Be mindful of your language, internally and externally. The words you choose to use when you think or speak will help to determine how you feel and how you behave. Use words to describe yourself and your circumstances that are empowering. Rather than allowing a negative thought such as, "My life is crap. I'm pretty sure it always will be," choose a thought such as, "There have been some things in my life that have been difficult for me, things that have made me feel sad. But I am working to become healthy." Or, "There have been some hard things in my life in the past, but I know I have the strength to deal with them. I have before, and I will again if I need to."

- Do not become your label. Have you been labeled as being depressed or anxious? Or perhaps your label is victim of post traumatic stress? Consider having no label at all, other than "learning, growing human." Changing your label will not negate the legitimacy of your pain, but it will open up the channels for growth and an opportunity to move forward from your pain.

- Eliminate from your vocabulary the phrase, "I am so stressed!" If you use other words that basically mean the same thing, eliminate them too.

- Set a positive tone. Sometimes when we come home at the end of a difficult day, we immediately launch into an account for our partner or friend that is all negative. Why not instead make a pact to share the positive first? I'm sure you will be able to find at least one positive thing, even if it is to say that the best part of the day is being able to come home and enjoy the company of your awesome partner.

- Remind yourself that you do not control another's thoughts or feelings or behaviour. Trying to make them change their thoughts or feelings or behaviour will not solve the problem. You do, however, control how you respond to them. Focus on your response and other problem-solving options, and your anxiety will decrease as you do so.

- Focus on small changes. Small changes may not solve the problem, but one step leads to another, and eventually a solution will be found. MOVEMENT CREATES MOVEMENT!

- Focus on goal setting and focus on what is possible. What steps can you take today that will eventually lead to resolution? (*Today* being the important word – don't wait to create that first bit of movement!)

- Repeat: stay focused on your own strengths and the strengths of others.

- Use a scale of one to ten to evaluate the seriousness of the problem. The other day I was delighted to see that my daughter is already using this with her three-year-old daughter. She said to my granddaughter, "Madeline, is this a big problem, a medium problem, or a small problem?" Madeline stopped her reaction (crying, frustrated) to think about what her mom had said to her. I'm not sure that Madeline actually understood the question that was being asked, but I could see this question helped her to focus on something other than her own angst.

- Use creativity to help you solve your problem. Paint or draw two pictures – one that shows how things look when this problem is in your life and one that shows how things look when this problem is not in your life. The very act of creating something tangible may help you to create steps to solve the problem.

- Use humour. Always use humour. You might wish to do some writing, or create a funny song or skit about what is going wrong. Perhaps you are taking yourself too seriously, and having a good laugh at your own expense will relieve some stress. I can't say enough about having a sense of humour when things are going wrong. I learned that from my grandmother, Gudrun, and her sisters who laughed when times were tough, laughing especially at themselves. It helped them to cope and move forward. I personally like to make up an "I've Got the _____ Blues" song, inserting whatever word fits the occasion, and then really ham up the delivery. I do it when I'm all by myself and somehow, it makes me feel better.

Sometimes doing something absurd and ridiculous will help you to feel less anxious. I remember reading about a ceremony that Jamie Sams, author of *Earth Medicine*, called Heyokah Moon Medicine. This ceremony is about using humour to help you handle your challenges. A few people gather for the ceremony, go into the back yard and drop their drawers, and…yes, moon the world. If you decide to give it a try, you might even want to gather a few friends to do it with you – you could be The Mooners Gang!

The Seven Steps of Solution Focused Problem Solving

You may wish to practice some solution focused problem solving right now. Think of a problem that is giving you a challenge, and work through the following steps:

1. Clearly and concisely identify the problem. You can't resolve an issue that is unclear to you. Write a brief description of the problem in one or two sentences. Use the words *how* or *what*; avoid the words *why* and *what if* - they are too open-ended, and likely to produce anxiety. (While you're at it, make sure that this issue is *yours* to solve, and that you have a measure of control over the solution.)

2. List all possible solutions. Think broadly but don't over-think. Get as many ideas down on paper as you possibly can, even if some of them sound a little bit ridiculous.

3. Spot and rule out the obvious no-goes. Choose the best solution to try. Recognize that the solution you try may not be the final answer to the problem, but could be a stepping stone to the right solution.

4. Make a plan and do it. Plans are not useful if they are never put into action. Just do it.

5. Evaluate the outcome. Did you partially or completely solve the problem? Did you learn something? Did you discover anything about other possible solutions?

6. If you didn't solve the problem, or even a piece of the problem, repeat the process. Repeating the process doesn't mean you've failed. It doesn't mean you should become anxious. It means that you have begun to clarify the real nature of the problem you're tackling. When you try things one step at a time, it prevents you from staying stuck. MOVEMENT CREATES MOVEMENT!

7. Don't be afraid to make a decision. I remember when I was in my thirties, and I started a new job, one that I believed was beyond my knowledge and credentials. I didn't have the appropriate experience for this job, and I was feeling quite intimidated. One really important aspect of my position was to make policy decisions. I felt incapable of doing this task, because I was afraid that I would make the wrong decision. My boss kept saying to me, "Make a decision! What's the worst that can happen?"

    At the time, I was a very accomplished what-iffer, and I could come up with all sorts of negative and terrifying scenarios as to what might go wrong. I eventually learned, though, that no decision I made was going to cause utter disaster. It was a huge relief to know that I could make a decision based on the experience and knowledge that I *did* have, and that no matter what I decided, it would be okay. My boss kindly let me know that he would have my back if I made a less than perfect decision, and that was all I needed to take the leap.

Remember this:

**IF YOU FOCUS ON THE PROBLEM, YOU WILL FIND
THE PROBLEM.**

**IF YOU FOCUS ON THE SOLUTION, YOU WILL FIND
THE SOLUTION.**

CHAPTER EIGHTEEN
Boundaries are Beautiful

When it comes to lowering your anxiety levels, boundaries are a truly beautiful thing. Here's how it works: when we do not have healthy boundaries in place, we'll most likely act in a way that is incongruent with our core beliefs. Guess what happens then? Our anxiety ratchets up.

How do we stray from our core beliefs and why? Why do some of us have good boundaries in place, and some of us do not? There are many whys, and I suggest that if you are moving away from your core beliefs and the things that are important to you, you may want to look into the whys for you. Are you afraid of hurting someone's feelings? Are you afraid of making someone uncomfortable? Do you not feel valuable enough to advocate for yourself?

The hows are a bit more straightforward. Let me share a few examples of how you might demonstrate to others that you do *not* have good boundaries. Perhaps you say yes, when what you really want to say is a resounding no. Have you ever done that, and then felt angry or resentful when it came time to do the thing you didn't really want to do in the first place?

Maybe someone is behaving in an unkind or disrespectful manner toward you, and you don't know how to get them to stop. As a result, day by day, the light of your self-esteem grows a little dimmer. Perhaps you're unable or unwilling to say what you think and feel or want and need. Maybe you've never learned from anyone how to do that. Or maybe, just maybe, you don't feel valued or feel that you have the right to advocate for yourself when someone is belit- tling or demeaning you. Because of that, you aren't *getting* what you want and need; your feelings are not being acknowledged and appreciated.

Maybe you're just a really kind soul who wants to empower others and befriend others, but because of the other's drama-filled life, you're being taken advantage of and hurt in the process. Maybe you're afraid to rock the boat, or you might be feeling powerless in a certain situation, because you believe that you have to change another person's behaviour to fix things. Now that you know that you're not going to change *their* behaviour, what are your options?

Good Boundaries: What They Are, and What They Are Not

My thinking around boundaries has been influenced by the writings and teachings of many. If you are having issues with the setting and maintaining of good boundaries, I would suggest that you have a look at Melody Beattie's book, *The New Codependency: Help and Guidance for Today's Generations*. She has an excellent section on boundaries that has been helpful to me.

Over the years, I've explored not only the positive value of bound- ary setting, but also how to set and maintain boundaries. I now practice boundary setting faithfully. Am I one hundred percent effective? No, but then again, I'm a work in progress, and that's okay. What I have found is that my life is much simpler and has much less anxiety when I set and maintain healthy boundaries. I'm all for simplifying things.

What have I learned? I've learned that good boundaries are not something that our husband, mother or best friend establish for us, and they aren't limits that we set because someone else tells us we should do it. Both of these types of limits would be external to us, and good boundaries always originate from within. In other words, it must be your idea.

Good boundaries are never angry, empty threats. We've all made an angry, empty threat in the heat of the moment. But we all know where that leads, don't we? An angry, empty threat is completely without value, because when we make it, we usually have no intention of enforcing or maintaining it. Quite often, the angry, empty threat is ridiculous to boot. Our brain simply doesn't function optimally when we are in anger mode.

Good boundaries must have a limit that we are willing to enforce and maintain for as long as necessary. If we set a boundary and we don't enforce and maintain it, the boundary is of absolutely no value. It's important to be sure that when you're setting a boundary, it is actually something that you are *able* to enforce and that you have the stamina and means to maintain it. This is why we don't set boundaries when we are angry. We need to be able to think them through.

Good boundaries are never an attempt to control someone else's behaviour. Of course not, because we already know that we are not ever going to be able to control someone else's behaviour. Enough said.

Good boundaries are about letting people know, in the clearest way possible, what is okay with us and what is not okay with us. We make it clear as to where our line in the sand is. For many of us, particularly the people-pleasers, this one is difficult. We don't want to make anyone unhappy or uncomfortable. We would much rather make *ourselves* unhappy and uncomfortable... *and more anxious.*

The reality is, no one can disrespect us without our implied permission. When we're practicing people-pleasing behaviours, we are giving that very permission.

I began to think about enabling in a new way after reading one of Candace Plattor's blog posts. We enable someone else's negative or destructive behaviour because we're too uncomfortable with the notion of making them uncomfortable. In other words, we enable to try and tamp down our own anxiety. *It never works!*

Giving away our power to please another person does not end well. This action of giving away our power has to change, doesn't it, if we are going to create a life for ourselves that is less anxious – a life where we are able to tell the whole world that we value ourselves enough to advocate on our own behalf? Visualize yourself telling people what you will do if they don't stop mistreating you, and then visualize yourself doing it. That's pretty empowering, isn't it? What's even more empowering is actually *doing* it for real.

Good boundaries are about saying yes when we mean it, and saying no when we mean it. When you're unsure about whether you want to say yes or no, it's quite acceptable to say, "I don't know. I'll think about it and get back to you." I find that often when we don't do any of the above, what happens is that we become angry and resentful toward the person who is *making us* do something, when in fact they are not making us do anything at all. We simply have failed to be clear about our boundaries, and the responsibility for our disappointment rests clearly with us.

It is important to state again that boundaries concern our own behaviour, what we will do and what we won't do, and, as I mentioned previously, they are not an attempt to control someone else's behaviour. They offer the other person a choice as to how they will respond to our boundary. Here's an example. Let's say I have a friend who is continuously showing up at my house, late in the evening, drunk as a skunk, loud and gregarious. It upsets me, irritates me, and interferes with my own plans for an evening of solitude and a good book. I have two choices as to how I might respond. I can keep my mouth shut, feel angry, and begin to resent my friend, or I can set a boundary. Which do you think will help me to feel less anxious?

I might say to my friend, "I really appreciate your company when you're sober. But please don't come over when you're drinking." With this statement, I am not controlling my friend's behaviour. She can choose how she responds to the boundary I've set. She can stay away from me when she is drinking, or she can come over when she's sober. The choice is hers. The important point here is that by speaking my mind, by saying what is okay with me and what is not okay with me, I am consciously choosing to lower my own anxiety. Empowering, yes?

I believe that speaking out on our own behalf is the first step toward loving ourselves the way we need to be loved. We can speak on our own behalf with grace, dignity, clarity, and confidence, but this will not happen if we speak out in anger. Take the time to think it through, and then muster up your courage to be your own knight in shining armor. You won't regret it.

A Few Boundary Setting Tips

Setting boundaries takes practice, especially if you've never had boundary setting modeled for you or taught to you. You may find that once you begin setting boundaries, your first attempts are awkward and over the top. That's okay. In fact, it's okay to tell someone that you are learning to set boundaries; hopefully they will not be offended if you don't do it exactly right the first time or two.

The first thing to consider is clarity. If your boundaries are unclear to you, they will most certainly be unclear to others. Have clarity in your own mind as to what your own boundary is, and how you intend to state it. Saying, "You're drunk. You need to smarten up," might leave your friend confused as to why you're angry and out of sorts and confused as to how she is supposed to "smarten up."

Don't be pressured into giving an answer that you don't want to give. If you're unsure, ask for time to think about it, and tell the person when you'll get back to them with your answer. Remember, if you're put in a position that makes you feel uncomfortable, your anxiety will increase. This one makes me think of my own mom, who had great difficulty saying no when it came to helping out. She was a kind, compassionate, and giving woman, and felt an obligation (and the desire) to always say yes. Sometimes, she got really tired, and on very rare occasions, her fatigue bordered on resentment. I have to admit, in the past I have occasionally found myself walking in my mother's footsteps.

There is no need to explain or justify what you want or don't want, what you will or will not tolerate; in fact, to do so may weaken your statement and encourage all sorts of arguments from the other side. Excuses may weaken your power. Years ago, my friend and I laughingly came up with many excuses we could give to our clients if we didn't want to go and see them and deal with their problems (which was actually our job). I think my all-time favourite was, "My womb fell out on the bus ride to Red Deer." Of course, we never used these excuses, but we sure had fun coming up with them.

In my earlier years, it was often difficult for me to say no when I wanted to. My husband at the time would become frustrated with me, because either I couldn't say no, or if I did finally manage to say no, I had a hundred and one excuses as to why I had to say no. It took me many years to drop the long line of excuses, but I finally managed (most of the time) to say, "No, I can't do that for you." Simple, isn't it? With that simple action, you will experience much less anxiety! I have to admit, in full disclosure, that I *still* almost always apologize when I say no... "I'm sorry, I can't do it." But I'm Canadian. What do you expect?

It is important to mention here that having healthy boundaries also means respecting other people's boundaries. My daughter is determined to teach her children that it is okay to say no, and that when another person tells you no, you need to respect that. I heard an interesting exchange recently between my five-year-old grandson and his three-year-old sister. It went like this:

Leon: Madeline, will you come and play with me?

Madeline: No, I don't want to.

Leon: But Madeline, I really want to play blocks with you.

Madeline: No, I don't want to.

Leon: But Madeline, I really like it when you play with me. It's really nice!

Madeline: (Yelling now) NO! I DON'T WANT TO!

Leon: (Also yelling now) MADELINE! I DON'T LIKE IT WHEN YOU REFUSE ME!

Of course, their mother saw this as a wonderful teaching moment. First, she complimented Leon for asking his sister nicely, and then she explained, once again, that no means no and that Leon must respect Madeline's right to say no. Madeline was listening to this exchange and was able to pick up that it is, in fact, okay for her to say no. Leon expressed what we all feel – we don't like it when someone refuses (or rejects) us, but despite that, he is learning to respect his sister's autonomy. When he is a young man, he will have no difficulty understanding that he must show respect to the people he is in relationship with. He will have these teachings about respect to guide him. And Madeline will have no difficulty saying no when she doesn't want to do something. She will know that not only is it okay for her to say no when she wants to, but that it is important for her to do so.

What if you're uncertain? Sometimes we aren't sure whether we want to say yes or say no. We may feel pressured to make a decision when we're not ready. It's absolutely okay to choose *not* make a decision – but own it when you do that. Don't shove the request under a rug and try to forget that someone has asked you to do something. It will seriously annoy them and continuously nag at you.

You may need to wait for more information and further clarity before you can make a sound decision, and that is okay! This is not to be mistaken with procrastination. I'm sure you know the difference. You'll feel it in the level of anxiety you're experiencing (it will be higher if you're procrastinating). At one time, my sister and I worked in the same office, and from time to time we would seek advice from each other about how to handle a situation. Always we would ask, "Do you have enough information to make a good decision?" It seemed, more often than not, that some information was indeed lacking and a good decision could not be made for that very reason.

It's important to mention that good boundary setting also includes being able to say what you *do* want and need and what you like. How else will people know? When you are able to advocate for yourself, you will no longer feel like a victim. Empowering, isn't it?

When setting boundaries, it's important to unhook from spoken or unspoken anger and aggression. We've all been there. Hostility and resentment coming our way, sometimes with words, some-times with body language and facial expressions, or maybe it's the silent treatment. Refuse to connect to this negative energy! It can sometimes be as simple as saying, "I'm not going to do this with you," and walk away. I often tell couples who fight all the time to take turns doing this. Refuse to participate in the hostility, but always, always say that you want to meet again in half an hour (or any specific time) in the kitchen (or any specific location) to resume the conversation without anger. It's a good way to have a cooling off period without leaving your partner feeling abandoned.

If boundary setting involves people doing something differently, be specific about what you want or don't want to happen. For example, if your household finances are upsetting you and leaving you anxious, saying, "Dammit Harold! You spend too damn much money!" is not likely to help the situation. You and Harold will both feel a little more anxiety with those words. You might instead wish to say something along the lines of, "Harold, I'm feeling anxious about our money situation. I want to sit down with you tonight, or in the next couple of nights, to do a household budget. It's really important to me that we get our spending under control. I'd like us to reach an agreement as to how we're going to do that."

Boundaries are set with love and compassion, and with the expectation of a positive outcome for *both* people. Staying focused on the issue, rather than the person, is important. If you focus on the person, a dynamic is set in place where that person will feel the need to defend. If, however, that person knows that you're reaching out with love, and focusing on an *issue* of concern, you are much more likely to have a good response to your boundary.

I once worked with a client (we'll call her Stella) who was having a lot of anxiety about her mother's 'interference' when it came to giving unsolicited advice about her grandchildren. Stella did not wish to upset or offend her mother and had been saying nothing at all about how she was feeling – namely that she did not appreciate her mother's unsolicited advice and interference. Because she was saying nothing, her anger and resentment (and level of anxiety) grew to the boiling point. She inevitably exploded in anger, telling her mother that she didn't want to associate with her at all anymore. Her mother was heartbroken and Stella was too.

How might Stella have handled that differently? It is important, at the outset of *any* discomfort, to talk about how you're feeling, what you're thinking, and what you want and need. Don't wait until the boiling point. When you do talk about things, do it with love and compassion for the person you are talking to.

Stella might have said something like this: "You know, mom, I really love you, and I value all of your knowledge and experience when it comes to parenting issues. But it's important that I learn how to do these things on my own. Here's what I would like to do: I would like to handle things on my own, without your advice or guidance. When I feel that I can benefit from all of the things that you have learned, I'll ask you for advice or help. Would that be okay with you? I really think that this would free you up to enjoy being a Grandma and give me the opportunity to learn about being a mom." This statement could be the beginning of a really good conversation about the role they each play in the children's lives. And if Grandma doesn't stop interfering, a short reminder, such as, "Mom, that's my job," should suffice.

Again, I want to remind you that you are not setting boundaries in anger. If you think things through ahead of time, you'll find that there is no reason to raise your voice. You will speak with a quiet authority, because you know that you are doing what is right for you. Not only is it the civilized thing to do – it is also a great way to decrease your anxiety.

Boundary Setting Burps

Boundary setting burps are the little things that can happen when people are not accustomed to you advocating for yourself. What burps can you perhaps expect?

Testing. That's right – you may be tested, to see if you are serious. Setting a boundary is only half the battle. Maintaining it is the other half. If you have previously set a boundary, and it ended up being an empty threat, you can be *sure* that you and your boundary will be tested. The reality is, if you're not serious, your boundary won't be taken seriously either. Stick to your plan. Show someone you are serious by reinforcing that boundary over and over again. It's sort of like being on a diet. Losing the weight is only the beginning. Maintaining the loss can be the hard part, but it will also be absolutely rewarding for a lifetime.

One of the simplest illustrations of boundary setting is in our relationships with children. Dad sets a boundary. "Melissa, if you don't stop hitting your brother, you will get a time out!" Melissa continues to pummel her little brother, not caring about the threatened time out. Dad repeats himself. "Melissa, I'm warning you. Stop hitting your brother, or you're going to your room!" Pummelling continues. Dad, tired of making threats, becoming angrier, hollers, "Melissa!!! Stop this right now!" Melissa doesn't stop, and now her brother is yelling louder than Melissa. Giving up, Dad goes outside because he can't stand the noise anymore. What has Melissa learned? She's learned that Dad makes empty threats. No need to listen to him. She's also learned that the next time Dad tries to discipline her, all she needs to do is wait him out, and nothing – no consequences – will happen.

Another example of testing might be in a relationship between husband and wife. I had a couple in counselling once who were experiencing marital difficulties. We'll call them Jack and Jill. Jill had an alcohol problem, and their relationship was on the brink of dissolving because of it. Much of her time was spent out partying with friends, away from her husband and children. In the past months and years, Jack had threatened often that he would leave with the children if the situation didn't change. The situation didn't change, and he never left. Empty threats. During the course of our sessions, Jack decided that he was ready to stop making empty threats, and that he was actually going to leave Jill if she didn't stop drinking. He followed through on that decision and left. Jill was shocked and angry, and she stopped coming to our sessions. Some weeks down the road, when Jack and I finished our sessions, he was feeling more settled about his choice, and their children were definitely feeling more settled. Jill was still drinking and partying. While not the ideal outcome, there was more of a chance of happiness for Jack and the children, and maybe one day, for Jill as well.

If you have people in your world who tend to be obsessive (who find it hard to let things go), or who are dependent on you, or perhaps who are used to calling all the shots, they may be persistent in testing your sincerity. You can be equally as persistent in maintaining your boundary. It's that choice again – give in and let your anxiety run wild, or calmly maintain that boundary, knowing that in the long run, you will be more peaceful and much more empowered.

You may find that you feel guilty for saying things that people don't want to hear. My question to you is this: would you rather feel guilty (and learn how to let that guilt go) or would you rather feel anxious (and continue to feel anxious)? Know that you are doing nothing wrong by setting a boundary. It is a healthy action, and not anything to feel guilty about. Just let go of that guilt! People will adjust. They will learn to work within your boundaries. If they don't, you may need to decide whether they have a rightful place in your life or not. Something to think about, for sure. After all, it's your health, right? What are you willing to do to take care of yourself, to live a life without overwhelming anxiety?

You may wish to prepare yourself for anger when some people realize that you are serious about boundary setting. Their anger is simply another way of testing you. Remember, this anger will most likely dissipate. If it doesn't, you may find that parting ways is best for both of you.

Boundaries, healthy boundaries, are flexible. That means that they can change, depending on you, the situation, and the person you are dealing with. Pay attention to your own anxiety levels and adjust your boundaries accordingly.

I Think...I Feel...I Want...I Need...

When setting boundaries, it is important to monitor your thoughts and feelings and to share them clearly. Use the words "I think" and "I feel" when expressing yourself. Remember, feelings are not thoughts. Many people have difficulty with this, but in my counselling practice, I have found that men often have more difficulty than women when it comes to expressing feelings. We women are generally more comfortable expressing our feelings because of the way we have been socialized. Many men (and some women) sometimes mistake thoughts for feelings. When I say, "How do you feel about this?" my client might respond with, "I feel that she shouldn't have done that. It wasn't right." In this response, my client has given me his thought. His feeling, which he has not expressed, is much more likely to be something along the lines of, "I feel hurt that she did that."

Saying what we want and need is almost, well, selfish – isn't it? No, it is not. Saying what we want and need is not only healthy, it is also a gift to the person we are relating to. There is nothing more difficult (and anxiety producing) than trying to guess what someone thinks, feels, wants, or needs. All too often, we try to please others by doing what we think they want, with the end result that no one is happy. For example:

Maude: "Do you want to go out for dinner tonight?"

Harold: "Sure, okay, if you do."

Maude: "Okay, great! Where do you want to go?"

Harold: "Where ever you want is okay by me."

Maude: "Do you want to go at seven o'clock, or eight o'clock?"

Harold: "Either one."

Maude: "Great! I'll pick you up at 7:45."

Harold: "Yeah, okay, I'll try to be ready by then. Grumble, grumble, grumble."

Later

Maude: "I loved that restaurant! Let's go back again next week!"

Harold: (Feeling anxious and out of sorts) "You always love that kind of shit. I hate vegetarian food. And I was too freaking hungry by the time we got there, I didn't even feel good. Why do you always do this to me? Next time I'm going to stay home."

Maude: (also feeling anxious now) "I'm sorry Harold. You never said that you don't like vegetarian food, and I thought the time was okay with you. I'm really disappointed. I thought you would enjoy it."

You see what I mean. No one is happy.

When you're trying to figure out what kind of boundaries you need in your own life to lessen your anxiety, it's always important to ask yourself (and then share with others) what you think, what you feel, what you want, and what you need. It will help you to clarify what the boundary needs to be, and also reinforce the why of setting it. This communication clarification is also part of advocating for yourself and valuing yourself.

Good communication and clear boundary setting also helps to avoid the confusion and disappointment that surrounds unmet expectations. I saw a wonderful example of my daughter sharing her expectations with her husband several years ago. We were all together in the car, and the radio happened to mention something about Valentine's Day coming up. My daughter looked at her husband and said, "Hey, Russell, Valentine's Day is coming up." His response was rather disinterested. He is not keen on commercialized and profit-based expressions of affection because society has deemed it is the appropriate day to do so. He is much more interested in expressing his affection when it's his idea, his feeling. My daughter, however, was thinking that she wanted something special that Valentine's Day.

The conversation continued. "I'd like some flowers for Valentine's Day," said my daughter. "Oh?" said her husband, still not particularly interested. "Yes, I'd really love some daisies!" What happened then was really lovely. Her husband turned to her, looked her in the eye and said, "Oh! Okay, I can do that!"

The beauty of this exchange was that my daughter clearly expressed what she wanted, her husband heard her, and even though it's not necessarily *his* thing, he was happy to do something that would make her happy. Can you imagine if she had said nothing? She would likely have been disappointed or even angry when the day was unacknowledged and her feelings were overlooked. Her husband would have been oblivious as to why, setting up a recurring scenario of unmet expectation and disappointment every year following. How wonderful that this clear communication, being able to say, "I want this…" produced such excellent results. My daughter felt good about her husband's willingness to give her the daisies, and her husband felt good about giving them to her. Win-win.

Racoon Teaches Woman to Say No

I was in my mid-fifties when I really began to understand the value of boundary setting. Prior to that, I didn't have the first clue about what to do. I knew that sometimes I lost myself in other people, trying to please every single one of them. I also knew that I had great difficulty saying no. When I felt like I could help someone, or I could get the job done without fuss, or I might enjoy doing the thing, even if I didn't have any time whatsoever, I would say yes when I should have said no. I decided to learn how to say no.

As I often do, I turned to my dreams. I asked for a dream about boundaries, about saying no. This is the dream that came to me, that very night:

I dreamed that I was in a basement with my youngest sister, Beverly, and my two cats, Tut and Cleo. Right away I noticed a large, white milk bottle, about two feet high. Strange. Suddenly the milk bottle toppled over and began rolling swiftly towards me. For some reason, I was utterly terrified. I screamed.

The milk bottle made a sharp turn away from me, and it was rolling rapidly towards Tut and Cleo. I was really afraid for them and screamed again. I wasn't reacting effectively at all. Beverly calmly walked toward the milk bottle, stopped it, stood it upright, and put her hand inside of it. Then she unceremoniously pulled out a racoon. End of dream.

When I woke up, I was completely baffled. I had learned nothing about boundaries, and I wrote the dream off as a dud. It's never a good idea to do that. Just because you don't get the message from the dream right away, it doesn't mean there *is* no message. I went down the stairs to my living room, and began my daily routine. I put the coffee on and sat down with Jamie Sams' book, *Earth Medicine.* At the time, I was using this book as a sort of daily meditative reading. I love her insight and teachings. It was my routine to open the book at random and read whatever wisdom presented itself to me that day. You can imagine my shock, and at the same time my feeling of awe, when I opened the book to a story I had never seen before, called *The Racoon's Lessons.* The hair on the back of my neck literally stood up, and I got the goose bumps all up and down my arms and legs.

I began to read the story. I was really shocked when I realized that this was a story about saying no, and about taking care of yourself – basically a story about boundaries. Briefly, the story was this: There was a terrible fire in the forest, and Mama Racoon worked tirelessly, night and day, day and night, to take care of all of the creatures in the forest. The other racoons worried about Mama Racoon, because she worked tirelessly, for days on end, and she was close to collapse. Finally, between a state of dreams and consciousness, Mama Racoon heard the Earth Mother speak to her. The Earth Mother told Mama Racoon that there are consequences to giving all of your strength to the needs of others.

Of course, Mama Racoon learned her lesson well and changed her ways. She reminds us to give to the best of our abilities, but not to the extent that we destroy our own health and sense of wellbeing.

Now, when I am tempted to take on too much, when I have difficulty saying no, I remember Mama Racoon, and the very dramatic way her lesson unfolded for me. Because I am able to listen to my body, and listen to the teachings of Mama Racoon, my anxiety level is much lower.

CHAPTER NINETEEN
Love Yourself Gently

No amount of self-improvement will make up for a lack of self-acceptance, because if you are unable to accept yourself, warts and all, any improvement you make will never be enough. When we do not accept ourselves as learning, growing humans, our anxiety increases. We have two selves – the image we present to others and our true self. I believe that when these two selves begin to comfortably merge, we have reached a satisfactory degree of self-acceptance. When the two selves are not congruent, we have a breeding ground for anxiety. It has certainly been true in my life. When I am not following the path that is right for me, there is a little internal hum of anxiety that simply will not stop. I believe that this is true for most people, but not everyone hears the hum.

What is the key that unlocks self-acceptance? I believe it is when we accept that we are not perfect, that we are "good enough" – potentially stellar in some areas and challenged in others.

Self-acceptance, bringing our two selves into one, is how we begin to find our joy and contentment. There is a world of difference between searching for happiness outside of yourself and creating joy within yourself. The first can be given to you, and it can also be taken from you. The second is yours to keep forever. To create joy within, it is necessary for us to accept who we truly are. I don't mean that we shouldn't ever strive to better ourselves – indeed, we should. What I do mean is that at some point, we will need to accept that striving for perfection is not realistic and can in fact be detrimental to our growth and our happiness.

Following our internal joy means, among other things, focusing internally, making healthy choices, responding to the events and people around us rather than reacting, and recognizing who we really are.

Focusing internally – what do I mean by that? I have been self-reflective from a young age. When I was a young teenager, my best friend Brenda used to ask me how I could sit in my room and think about things and be content with my own company. She was very much a social connector and loved being with people. She still is a most talented and giving social connector, and although I love being with people, I am still content with my own company. Spending time alone in my young adulthood, and again in my fifties, gave me the space and energy to consider what was really important to me and how I wanted to live in the world.

Making healthy choices was essential for me in terms of learning who I really am. I stopped living in a marriage that was unhealthy for both my husband and I. I quit drinking alcohol and rediscovered my freedom to really engage with the world in a creative way. I stopped smoking cigarettes, and when I quit, it was like breaking out of jail – more freedom! I started to exercise and eat healthy food – a no brainer. I went back to university to learn. I rediscovered my *joy!*

By making all of these healthy choices, I began to respond in a more measured way to the people and events around me, rather than reacting to them (for the most part). As I said previously, I'm a work in progress, just as you are. The reality is, we will all be this work in progress every day for the rest of our lives.

How exactly do we go about discovering who we really are? For me, it was necessary to think back to when I was ten years old, the time in my life when I was the purest version of myself. At the age of ten, I was beginning to discover what I was passionate about, beginning to express my joy through music and creativity, beginning to recognize that I love to learn, and I was also beginning to recognize my compassionate self. From these four things – my passions, my love of learning, my creativity, and my compassion – the core of me was formed. I lost that core for many years, but when I began to look at my life, and make a conscious choice to live as my authentic self, it was necessary to return to the roots of me to discover what my authentic self actually was. I was delighted to discover that I was still in there.

I have a little exercise for you that you may find valuable. Find a journal – it can be an old scribbler you have at home, or a brand-new fancy journal from the store. Do some daily writing for ten days, focusing on the following questions:

- Who was I when I was ten years old? What did I care about? How did I spend my time? What excited me? (If you had a difficult or abusive childhood, go to the time in your life when you first discovered that you had some strengths and a time when you experienced some joy and then work from that period.)
- When, now, do I feel like I am the real me? When do I feel like I did when I was ten?
- When do I feel most energized and joyful?
- Who inspires me, and what inspires me?
- What do I feel most passionate about?
- How do I play?
- What makes me lose track of time and puts me *in the flow?*
- What makes me laugh? What breaks my heart?

- What did I have then, inside of me, that I don't have now? Do I want it back?
- What do I want to stand for?
- What do I have to give?
- What do I want to receive?

As you reach the conclusion of the ten day period, focus on the things that have the greatest impact on you. Let this be a first step to something new. You might be surprised where this exercise leads you.

We are learning, growing creatures who will make mistakes. Mistakes can be a burden we carry forever, or our biggest opportunity for growth. I have certainly made mistakes in my lifetime, and I like to think that for the most part, I've learned important lessons from them. I no longer berate myself for the things I've done wrong, and I no longer carry guilt about them. Guilt is such a waste of good energy, energy that can be used to learn and grow and give back to the people we love, the people we may have let down at some point. Why not choose to let go of guilt and use that energy to create joy? It really is a choice, and you get to make it.

In my twenties, when I was attending university, my friend and I practiced saying the phrase, "Love yourself gently," over and over again, to help us learn to deal with excessive feelings of guilt and other inadequacies. If we are able to love ourselves gently, as we would love our best friend, our self-talk will change dramatically. Why not give it a try?

I found a prayer/poem in a magazine many years ago. It was written by an anonymous (or unknown) author. The prayer is about our very humanity, and the idea that we do make mistakes, but we are learning and growing creatures, and that's absolutely okay.

When I discovered this prayer, I cut it out and taped it to my bathroom mirror. I read it aloud every single day, until one day I realized that I actually, finally, believed every word of it – not every waking moment of my life, but most moments. I have shared it with friends and with clients, and now I would like to share it with you. I give gratitude to the unknown author.

Daily Prayer of Acceptance

I accept myself completely.
I accept my strengths and my weaknesses, my gifts and my shortcomings.
I accept myself completely as a human being.
I accept that I am here to learn and grow, and I accept that I am learning and growing.
I accept the personality I've developed, and I accept my power to heal and change.
Today I choose to release _____ and I choose to embrace _____.

I accept myself without condition or reservation.
I accept that the core of my being is goodness and that my essence is love, and I accept that sometimes I forget that.

I accept myself completely, and in this acceptance
I find an ever-deepening strength.
From this place of strength, I accept my life fully and
I am open to the lessons it offers me each day.

I accept that within my mind are both fear and love, and
I accept my power to choose which I will experience as real.
I recognize that I experience only the results of my own choices.
I accept the times that I choose fear as part of my learning and healing process,

And I accept that I have the potential and the power in any moment to choose love instead.

I accept mistakes as part of my growth.
I am willing to forgive myself and give myself another chance.
And I commit myself to aligning my thoughts more and more each day with the Thought of Love.
I am Love's hands, voice, and heart on Earth.

I accept my own life as a blessing and a gift.
My heart is open to receive, and I am deeply grateful.
May I always share the gifts that I receive…fully, freely and joyfully.
I accept all that I was, all that I am, and all that I choose to become.

CHAPTER TWENTY
Clean Out the Clutter

This chapter may or may not apply to you. I tend to feel uneasy and anxious when my physical surroundings are in a state of disarray. I like to have things organized and at my fingertips. It's as if I have a little brain map that goes wonky when my environment is, for lack of a better word, wonky. Clutter tells me that my work is not done and distracts me from the very thing I should be focusing on.

Organization is something in my world that I can control, and that in itself is a de-escalator as far as anxiety goes. I'm going to share some of the decluttering tips with you that have helped me to create an environment that gives me the most peace. I have gathered these tips from various sources, most of them shared with me by friends and family. Some of them I learned on my own, when I experimented with downsizing and organizing.

Out of curiosity, I went on the Amazon site to see how many books have been written about this subject. There were 62 pages of books about decluttering, with about 16 books per page – almost a thousand books written about decluttering, just on the Amazon site! I guess this tells us that decluttering is on the minds of many people.

The tips are pretty much universal when it comes to the basics, and I've shared the tips that work for me.

Physical Declutter:

- Piles are painful: I tend to become uneasy when my filing pile gets too big and takes up too much space. I need to take this one step further though and add *shred it.* I tend to hang on to paper much too long, and I suspect that this is an age thing. I, along with many of my contemporaries, seem to like paper copies. My daughter and her friends are much more comfortable retaining copies of documents on their computers, or not at all. Shred everything you can, and then recycle the shredded paper.

- Don't put it down – put it away. You may feel like this takes too much time, but in reality, it will save you time and frustration down the road.

- Get rid of items you don't use or enjoy. I have always loved *my stuff*, but I find that as I age, I have less desire for stuff. It has really helped me to remember that when I am giving things away, they are usually going to people who need them and want them. They might even love them like I do.

- Organize with bins, hooks, containers, and racks. I get great satisfaction out of doing this one. I guess it appeals to my sense of order.

- Set goals for each day, but not too many goals. Make it achievable. I'm learning to do this one. I was inspired by my nephew, Corey Cottrell, who has a Goals and Gratitude group, where the focus is on achievable goals and the expression of daily gratitude. It is an amazing source of support for many people who participate – a real tribe. You can find a link to his group at the back of this book.

- Designate handy spots for the things you use the most. Anxiety can be stirred up over small things – such as lost articles.

- Have a spot in each room for items that normally end up as clutter in that room. Use that spot.

- Make a to-do list. This one is so effective that sometimes I add things to the list that I've already done, just so I can cross them off. My brain is really happy when I do that!

- "Some day I will do this." No. We're not procrastinating any more. Pick a day, pick a time, write it in your daily planner, and do it. Or decide that you're never going to do it, and cross it off your list permanently.

- Speaking of daily planner, buy a book, a wall calendar, or use your phone or computer to keep track of the things you want or need to do, in order of priority. When you've done them, congratulate or reward yourself with a big cheer. No, you don't need chocolate as a reward, although maybe for the really tough things it would be appropriate.

- Something new in – something old out. Easier said than done, but a good balance to aspire to.

- Break big tasks into smaller tasks. This is important when it comes to decreasing anxiety. All too often we feel over-whelmed by the huge number and scope of tasks ahead of us and become anxious as a result. Once a task is broken down into do-able pieces, our anxiety levels will decrease accordingly.

- Don't put your life in storage. Use your "precious things" and enjoy them. For years, I had my mom's Limoges china in a box in storage, because I didn't want to break any of it. (You know…what if?) I did the same with my mom's and grand-mother's linens, tablecloths, etc. They had embroidered them, and they are precious to me. One day, I realized how foolish I was being. I felt sad that these beautiful things had not seen the light of day for years. I brought them all out of storage, and they are now being used with great joy. As an added bonus, I have a lot less anxiety about *too much stuff* in storage.

- Recycle paper you won't be reading. Recycle absolutely everything you can. While you're at it, reduce and re-use. Buy less stuff. You'll definitely feel less anxious about your finances.

- Set yourself up with e-bills and e-payments whenever you can. I wasn't sure that I would like this, but now I wouldn't be without it.

- Use your shredder regularly (the operative word here being *regularly*). Several months ago, I was down and out with the flu and incapable of doing much of anything. I lugged file boxes into my living room, sat on my couch, and shredded paper. I swore that this would become an annual or semi-annual thing. It is almost time to do it again and I'm pleased to report that I have recruited my young grandson to help me. Not only does it help me get rid of paper, it gives us something to do together and gives him a new skill that he can be proud of.

- Do small chores right away – for example, fold your sweater and put it away. Don't lay it on your rocking chair. (Note to self.) By doing this, you get the added bonus of creating some physical movement, which will also help with your anxiety.

- Do you have four hundred emails in your personal or work in-box? Commit to clearing new emails out daily (or within 48 hours at the latest), plus 20 more, until you are all caught up. Then continue to clear them out daily. Remember, if you need to answer a difficult email, procrastination will only make it more difficult.

- Be aware of the difference between your wants and needs. As I age, I truly desire to consume less, to leave a lighter footprint. As I move in this direction, I find I have less clutter (and less anxiety) in my life.

- Clothing – what have you not worn for a year? Are you likely to wear it next year? If not, someone else will be happy to have it.

- Create labeled file folders. I don't know what I'd do without my file folders. I love them. I lose fewer important pieces of information when I make the effort to put it in a file. I reuse files all the time, and that way it doesn't become expensive. When the file folders get to the point where they really aren't re-useable any more, I get out my stapler and make a home for the Batman and Superman cardboard figures that my grandson loves.

- Have your family participate in clean up before bed. That's another thing that is working really well for my daughter and son in law. They have instituted clean up time for their children, who are aged 5 and 3. This happens before supper, and the kids now expect it and do it without complaint (most days). Toys in the toy box, colours in the colouring dish, books in the book case. Living room clean! I love that my grandchildren are learning at an early age to attend to their own clutter.

- Eliminate toy clutter. Every few months, my daughter cleans out the toys the kids are no longer interested in. She takes them to a children's second-hand store and allows each of her children to pick out a new/used toy. The added bonus here is that you are teaching your children to consume responsibly. Word of advice – do your final purging after the kids have gone to bed.

- Do you use your plastic containers that don't have lids? If not, recycle them.

- Keep a bag or box in your laundry area that is designated as your give away space. When it's full, take it where the items are needed most.

- Give gifts that don't take up space. My daughter and her husband are minimalists. They don't clutter up their home.

They enjoy gifts that involve experiences, as opposed to space-gobbling gifts. I am training myself, slowly, to remember this at gift-giving time. Normally, at Christmas and on birthdays, I enjoy wrapping gifts and giving *stuff*. For the past two years I've given my daughter and her husband a monthly date. This gift involves some money and baby-sitting, with the proviso that they take turns planning an adventure date – something they have not tried before. They are really enjoying it, and I get awesome time with my little ones. This sounds like a repeat for next year.

If nothing else, I really urge you to pick five or six of the ideas above, do them, and see if your anxiety lessens over time. If it does, add five or six more. De-cluttering certainly helps me and may work for you too.

Physical de-cluttering is the place to start. As you find your home becoming less cluttered, I would wager that you will become more interested in de-cluttering mentally and emotionally as well. While you're at it, you may find yourself wondering if there is perhaps some spiritual de-cluttering that needs to happen too. Think of it this way – you are creating the space you need for peace in your life.

Decluttering mentally, emotionally, and spiritually will mean different things for different people. This is what it means to me:

Mental Declutter:

Sometimes I find that my mind gets overwhelmed with information it doesn't need, with learning that no longer benefits me, or with thought processes that do not work in my best interests. When this happens, it's time to re-evaluate and discover what I can change or let go of, to clarify my thinking. We make better decisions when we're thinking clearly. Let me give you an example. It's been a joy writing this book but there are times when I realize I don't know a lot about editing or formatting. I am grateful that my daughter, Jennifer, will step in and handle those tasks for me, and then I can let go of that worry. I definitely have learned to ask for help when I need it! In this way, I have more room for the things I really enjoy. I find as I age that I am more open to the idea of allowing information to come in and go out as it will. I need not retain every little bit of it.

Emotional Declutter:

Sometimes we need to re-evaluate our relationships to see if they are still a positive force in our lives. You may wish to look closely at your core relationships and see if there might be some positive changes that can be made. Do you need to set boundaries? Do you wish to spend more time together, or perhaps less time together? Are you happy with the quality of the time you have together? How might you create change that benefits you both?

Do you have close friends who are no longer putting in the effort that friendships require? Are some of your relationships one-sided? How might you create change to make these relationships more balanced? Perhaps you have a relationship that has become toxic. Is it time to cut the cord?

Look at your peripheral relationships. Are there some you want to let go, and others that you want to explore a little more?

What about your emotions? Do you sometimes feel overwhelmed with negative emotion? Are you surrounded by people who are negative, critical, unkind? Do you want to bring more positive people (and situations) into your life in a deliberate manner? Do you know how to do this?

Are you lonely? Is your life full of busy activity that does not give you the emotional connection that you need? According to one study, only 11% of men feel that they have someone in their lives that they can turn to in a crisis. Sadly, this means that 89% of men feel that they have *no one* to turn to in a crisis! Is it perhaps time to open up to a deeper intimacy with someone you care about?

Are you sometimes held back by fear or a sense of inadequacy? How might you let that go and instead choose to act with confidence and love?

Spiritual Declutter:

Are you stuck in a rut spiritually? Do you belong to a religious organization that no longer meets your needs? How might you meet those needs in a different way, or with a different organization? Perhaps you might be able to instigate some positive change in the organization you are a part of?

Perhaps you are not religious, and spirituality for you is more about meaning and purpose. You may wish to consider whether the meaning and/or purpose in your life have become clouded with confusion or perhaps need some updating. As we grow, we change, and our needs change too. Perhaps a vision board would help you to clarify what you want and need spiritually and how you might set about achieving that.

Maybe you have lost connection with the earth or with the people you love. Perhaps carving out time for reconnection is important for you. No matter which areas of your life you choose to declutter, you will find a sense of freedom as you *let go of stuff.*

A Final Word about De-Cluttering

Balance. That is my final word. While you are in the process of de-cluttering, and enjoying the results, take care to not overdo it. Do not let physical de-cluttering become an obsession, to the point where you and your family are tied to an exacting, unrelenting de-cluttered lifestyle. Your home needs to be lived in, loved, messed up, and generally enjoyed. Clean-up time is for clean-up time. The rest of the time, enjoy!

As you re-evaluate the mental, emotional, and spiritual clutter in your life, the same ideas apply. Look carefully at changes that might be positive for you, but as you move in a new direction, ensure that you don't throw the baby out with the bathwater unless you are looking for revolutionary change. Keep in mind, this revolution might be exactly what you need.

CHAPTER TWENTY-ONE
Meditation – Much Ado about Nothing...Or Is It?

Yes, there is much to be said about the power of reaching a state of nothingness. I have not managed to do that, but my hat goes off to anyone who can empty their head of chatter and distraction. For many years, I believed that I would be incapable of meditating, because the chatter in my head kept interrupting me. I thought that the goal was to reach a state of blissful nothingness, an impossible task for me. Rather than accept defeat, I decided to learn about meditation. For a while I meditated with some Buddhist monks. I read about meditation and asked questions. I tried to practice.

Over time I learned that the goal is to focus, become aware of the distractions, and refocus – over and over again. This is considered successful meditation; to notice that you are distracted, to be friendly towards that distraction, to have no judgement about it, gently let the distraction go, and then re-focus. It can be as simple as focusing on your breath...in...out...in...out. Before you tune out here because you believe that you're too busy to meditate, I must tell you that experts say that five minutes, even one minute, will begin to create positive changes in your brain, to help you respond, rather than react, to the world around you.

Recent research suggests that practices such as yoga and meditation actually create positive changes at the molecular level and can change the way our genetic code is expressed, reversing the effect that stress and anxiety have on the body. In addition, you might also find that the practice of meditation can be quite pleasant, and what was once a one-minute effort for you may well become a five-minute effort, and that five-minute effort may become a ten-minute enjoyable experience.

Meditation is about being aware and being mindful. It is about focus and refocus, and you can focus on anything at all. You may wish to meditate on the sight of a bird in a tree or the sound of the wind. You may wish to meditate on the taste of your orange or a feeling of calmness. You can even do a washing-dishes meditation or a holding-the-baby meditation, activating your senses to do so. It simply means bringing your full attention to whatever it is you are doing, and when you become distracted, bring your attention back to that original focus.

I have found that I really like mantra meditations, and that they have a calming effect on my mind and my body. I would like to share two meditations with you that have been helpful to me. In case you're wondering, "What the heck is a mantra?" I will share with you what I know.

The word mantra simply means chant or refrain; in other words, it is something we say over and over again. It's a sound with a pleasant vibration. The mantra we used when I learned a meditation in my yoga class was "So Hum," meaning "I am that I am." It's good to choose a word that does not create a picture in your mind. For example, if I choose the words big cheese, I will picture a big piece of cheese every time I say or think the words. But by all means, feel free to choose whatever mantra you wish. I was also taught that I could sing "So Hum," and it has a beautiful tune.

One night, I decided to practice a group "So-Hum" singing meditation. I invited three other women to join me in my home. What an experience! I was told that singing it 93 times was the goal. For the life of me, I can't recall why 93 times, or what that even means, but I wanted to do it anyway. We each had a small bowl with 93 popcorn kernels in it. We sat in a circle on the floor, and sang the So Hum song over and over again. Each time we finished the refrain, we would take one tiny kernel from our own bowl and place it in a larger bowl in the centre. In that way, we could continue singing the verse 93 times without having to concentrate on counting. The experience was absolutely magical. I don't think I can adequately express the phenomenal sense of peace and stillness I felt when we were finished, all of us at precisely the same moment.

Why might we want to do this? Meditation has so many proven benefits. It will help us use our breath, quiet our mental activity, and bring us to a place of restful awareness. It will help us to slow our heart rates, lower our blood pressure, quiet our breathing, (especially that shallow breathing we do when we're anxious) and it will lower our stress hormone levels. Meditation will also help us become more centred, less reactive and more responsive to stressful situations, *less anxious,* less depressed, more creative, and less habitual in all aspects of our lives. Wow! This sounds like it might be something important to learn, doesn't it?

Meditation How-To

I am definitely not a meditation expert, but I'm going to share with you what I know and what I have experienced, in case you have never meditated before. For a more in-depth and enjoyable look at meditation, if you are a beginner, I recommend you check out the book *Meditation for Fidgety Skeptics: A 10% Happier How-To Book* by Dan Harris and Jeff Warren, with Carlye Adler. Harris was an ABC news anchor (after reporting from war zones for many years) when he had a panic attack on air, and went in search of help. He found meditation. He has a sense of humour and addresses, as the title suggests, the many concerns of those among us who are skeptical about the value of meditation. I previously mentioned Thich Nhat Hanh's book, *A Pebble for Your Pocket.* In this book, Hanh provides some breathing meditations as well as mantra meditations that you might enjoy.

Because it is difficult for me to quiet my mind chatter, I choose a **mantra meditation**. I find that the following steps work well:

- Find a quiet place where you will not be disturbed for 20 to 30 minutes. (I recommend you start with 5 minutes and gradually work your way up.) Turn off all your communication devices. It may help you to have a stop watch or timer of some sort to ding when it's time to quit, thus preventing yourself from peeking at the clock all the time. Sit comfortably with your back supported. (You don't have to sit cross-legged.)

- Take a few deep breaths (deep enough that you can see your hand rise and fall as it sits on your belly button). Allow the tension to be released from your body. (Be aware of where you are holding your tension – shoulders? Neck? Jaw? Back? Legs?)

- Close your eyes and simply become aware of the activity of your mind. Notice how your thoughts come and go without any effort on your part.

- Observe the in-flow and the out-flow of your breath without attempting to consciously influence the rate or depth of your breathing, neither resisting nor anticipating any particular experience.

- Silently repeat the mantra "So-Hum" with your breathing. Think "So" with the in-breath and "Hum" with the out-breath. (Of course, use the mantra of your choice.)

- Continue the meditation until the time you have set aside is completed. Allow your awareness to float freely, and after a couple of minutes, resume your daily activities.

You may find from time to time that your attention is drifting away from the mantra and you're thinking another thought. Or you may become aware of sounds or activity in your environment. Or maybe you'll feel something in your body that wants your attention. That's okay. Gently return your attention to the mantra and continue your "So-Hum" breathing.

Some people fall asleep when meditating. That's okay too. If you're falling asleep, you obviously need the rest. Take advantage of this quiet time and do what your body needs you to do. When you awaken, try to spend at least five minutes on the mantra before resuming your daily activities.

Another meditation I quite enjoy is one that I call the **gratitude meditation,** because it allows me to focus on the gratitude I feel for someone I love, for my own body, and for my own breath. This one only takes a few short minutes, and you could even do it a couple of times a day – maybe upon awakening in the morning and before falling asleep.

- Sit quietly and comfortably, with arms and palms open. Close your eyes.

- Place your attention on your heart, and begin to reflect – who am I grateful for?

- Think of someone you love. It can be someone who is in your life now, or someone who is no longer with you. Bring the image of that person into your awareness and then into your heart.

- Imagine a great healing light filled with peace and warmth surrounding you and your loved one.

- Bring awareness to your breath; breathe deeply into your belly, letting the breath go with ease.

- Relax. Be at peace.

- Open your eyes when you are ready.

This is a beautiful meditation to do when you are feeling anxious about a loved one, perhaps stewing about *their* issue. You know that you do not control what you cannot control. Sending love and support in this way will help you to feel less anxious and will energetically and lovingly support the person you are worried about.

Meditation for Children

Kerry Lee MacLean wrote a wonderful book for children (and adults) to help them learn how to deal with anger, sadness, and anxiety by utilizing breath work and meditation. *Peaceful Piggy Meditation* is often requested by both of my grandchildren, and in the case of the elder of the two, it has been helpful to him when it comes to creating a little more peace at bedtime. Honing the skills of breath-work and meditation is going to take a bit of practice though. I recently asked my grandson if he had been able to get to sleep easily and he said, "Well, I was peaceful going up the stairs, but when I got to my bedroom, the peace just escaped from me." Upon further questioning, I learned that his peace just wanted to come out and play.

You can create your own meditations to do with your children. Many years ago – over 60 years! – my grandmother taught me a bedtime prayer/poem that I now use for a goodnight meditation with my five-year-old grandson, Leon. Ours is a talking meditation, rather like the God blesses that my mom taught me for bedtime prayers. We start by saying goodnight to various animals – usually animals who have cropped up in our bedtime stories, or animals that we have seen that day. Leon has become inventive and often includes his own choices. We then move to the elements, often saying goodnight to the sun, the moon, the stars, the trees, or the rivers. We might then say goodnight to an author or painter we have discovered that day.

One day, Leon and I read a book called *Relatives with Roots* by Leah Marie Dorion, a very talented Canadian Metis painter and author. This book is a beautiful story about Metis women's connection to the land, and one young girl's special connection to her grandmother. Leah's art work in the book is nothing short of stunning. During our goodnight meditation, we said goodnight to all the authors in the world who write books for children and make beautiful art for us all, and then I said goodnight especially to Leah Dorion. Leon immediately followed that with, "And we *love* her." At that moment, I knew that our goodnight meditation was important to both of us.

As we move through our goodnight meditation, we say our good-nights to our people, and it goes like this.

Goodnight to all the moms in the world, especially Jennifer Barrett (his mom).
Goodnight to all the dads in the world, especially Russell Nadin (his dad).
Good night to all the little sisters in the world, especially Madeline (his sister).
Goodnight to all the Grandmothers in the world, especially Nanny, Nona, and Grammie...

We cover several relatives, and often single out some of them by name. And then we conclude by saying this poem together, that my Grandmother said with me whenever I had a sleep-over at her house:

Goodnight, goodnight,
Fast flies the light.
But still great love
Will flame above,
And make all things bright.
Goodnight, goodnight.

There is something about doing ritual with children, tending to the sacred, that fills me with great peace and joy. I must say, though, that as my grandson recognizes his own power to create, the process becomes less meditative and more hilarious. Recently he's been determined to incorporate a dog or a cat into the narrative ("Fast flies the dog...") Nevertheless, I feel that we are meditating together in our own way, and for us, it is a beautiful thing.

CHAPTER TWENTY-TWO
Visualize Yourself to Newness

I can't say enough about the power of my brain and your brain when it comes to visualizing outcomes. Through the years, I have learned about the positive impact that deep trance work and visualization can have on shifting the narrative, helping people to let go and move beyond their trauma and grief. I have learned to use the power of my own brain and recognize that other people can also use the power of their own brains to create an actual change in the way they think and feel, and ultimately, how they behave.

If you have any doubts about the power of visualization to create something good in your life, just think for a minute about the power of visualization to create something bad in your life. Most of the time when you're worrying about something or feeling anxious about some person or some event in your life, you're visualizing all of the negative possibilities. You may not be conscious of doing that, but that is exactly what you are doing, and it is powerful, is it not? Let's focus on how you might use visualization to create more calm in your day.

Create Safe Space

One of the first things I would encourage you to do is to create, in your mind, a safe place. This will be a place where you can go when you are feeling anxious. The first time I created a safe place for myself was when I was a little girl. There was a picture hanging on the wall in my Grandmother's living room of a mountain, a lake, a shoreline, and some trees. I don't know why, but I longed to go there and be inside of that picture. I felt so peaceful when I was looking at it. In hindsight, this was indeed a safe place for me to disappear into. As an adult, I've learned that having a safe place to go in our minds is an important part of being able to cope with intense anxiety and flare-ups of our traumatic experiences.

My choice of a safe and meditative place as an adult has been a wheat field. I am a farmer's daughter, and for me, being on the land under a wide-open sky has always been not only safe, but utterly peaceful. I'm going to use all of my senses to create that place, to share with you a blueprint to help you create your own safe space. Keep in mind that this space that you picture in your mind can be either real or entirely imagined.

Seeing: I am standing on the land, in the middle of a wheat field. The wheat is about two feet high, thick, golden in color. The wheat is not moving. Everything is still. Above me is a wide, wide blue sky. The sun is overhead, slightly to my left. There are no buildings or vehicles nearby and no other humans. I can see forever.

Hearing: Crickets. I hear crickets chirping. I also hear a quiet buzz – insects singing their song. Otherwise, silence.

Smelling: I smell the earth. Rich, slightly musty, lush, loamy. That earthy smell. The air is clear and fresh.

Touch: I bend to touch the wheat. It feels like… wheat. How to explain that sensation? The smooth slipperiness of the stalk, the bumps on the head. I touch the earth – warm to my fingers, the land warmed by the sun above. Smooth, rich.

Taste: I'm not going to eat the dirt, but I do reach down and take a wheat kernel into my mouth. I chew. It's hard. Really tiny. The flavour? Well, it tastes like wheat.

My attention turns to where I am in this picture. At first, I am standing and gazing at the scene around me. Eventually, I spread my blanket, and lay on the ground, and feel the sun on my face. I am still. I am safe.

Now it's your turn. Close your eyes, and begin to visualize your own safe place. Know that when you want to, you can go to this safe place any time you feel the need. Your brain has created it, and it is yours for as long as you wish. If you want to make changes to that space, your brain will do that for you too. I encourage you to hold on to all of your sensory images and especially how you feel when you are present in that moment. It is this feeling that you will want to recall when you need to feel safe.

Just Put That Stuff on the Bus

I was recently involved in a Facebook discussion about anxiety and was struck by one woman's use of visualization to send her anxieties packing. Theresa Lutz, who has at times led group meditations or visualizations, told me that she first got the idea for dealing with her anxiety in this way while at a yoga class. Theresa has generously given me permission to share this with you, just as I hope that all of you will share your own strategies with others who might benefit. The yoga instructor at one point said to Theresa, about her anxieties, "Just put that stuff on the bus!"

Theresa decided that was a great idea. In her meditation, or visualization, she would take herself to a park bench and wait for the bus to come. The doors of the bus were on the side away from her, and she would visualize her anxieties disappearing around the bus to get in the door on the far side. She would then see her anxieties through the bus window, and they would sometimes wave goodbye as the bus drove away. The anxieties were permanently relocated.

At times Theresa worried that she might accidentally send something away that she still needed to attend to (tasks that were mounting up and beginning to feel overwhelming, creating anxiety for her). Once again, her visualization was happy to accommodate her needs. She was able to create a pond, and all of the tasks that she needed to do in future became ducklings who would happily swim around until Theresa was ready to go and deal with them. She felt quite happy watching them swim, because in so doing, her worries became less burdensome. She delighted herself by making them, on one occasion, get in a line. I really love that Theresa was able to create this beautiful visualization for herself. What is so awesome is that if this visualization is done often enough, it will create a signal in her brain so that eventually she won't even need to conjure up the whole scenario each time. She can quite simply say to her worry, "Get on the bus!" and her brain will get the message.

Talking to our Cells

All of us have had, from time to time, a health concern. We may have endlessly ruminated on it, creating catastrophic conclusions in our minds where none existed. You know that whatever it is you are ruminating on is basically out of your control, right? You control your thoughts, feelings, and behavior, (yes, you can control medical decisions about your own body) and how you respond to this health crisis and the people involved in it. You can visualize good outcomes or bad outcomes.

Why not give your body the love and support that will encourage a positive outcome? Let the catastrophic thinking go and, in its place, visualize your cells busy at work repairing themselves. What do they look like? Where are they in your body? What are they doing in there? What do they need besides a whole lot of love? Give them everything you've got to give. When you find the cells that refuse to repair, and are harmful to you, think about where you might like to send them. Perhaps they are going to put on a pair of roller skates and zoom right out of your body, off into the sunset.

Then perhaps you may wish to turn your attention to the parts of your body that are working hard on your behalf. It may be that your immune system is giving everything its got, and it could use a little bolstering. Maybe you'll want to envision what your immune system looks like. Make it something concrete, place it in your body, perhaps give it a name and a personality, and then become its cheering squad. Watch it do the good work on your behalf.

This is your visualization. It will take your time and energy to create what works for you, and while you're doing that, you'll have much less time to feel anxious.

Rock Around the Clock

If anxiety is much like singing the blues, I'd like to suggest that you rock and roll for a change. Rocks are wonderful little... creatures? I have loved rocks since my early childhood. I remember going into my father's field where I slowly but surely found and then carted home one rock after another, until I had a nice little collection. I put them all under my bed, and over time, they all turned white. I have no explanation for that, but always felt comforted knowing that they were there. Today, for my grandchildren and I, rocks take on a life of their own. I have bowls and baskets of rocks everywhere. They are grounding, and my grandchildren seem to know that this is so, without me telling them. Almost every time they come to visit me, we sit and go through a bowl of rocks, admiring them and talking about them. Even Madeline, at the age of three, will now tell me when she thinks a rock is "beautiful" or "feels good." Apparently, my rocks *are* actually magical. They are slowly disappearing from my home and my daughter tells me that they have begun reappearing at her home, in pants pockets and in her washing machine. I love that Leon and Madeline feel the way I do about rocks!

A simple way to deal with children's worries, after you've talked them over and done what you can to alleviate them, is to let your child place the worry inside the rock. First let them describe the worry to you, and then describe what the space inside the rock looks like. Talk about how the worry will be at home there. Let them know that for now the rock will take care of the worry. Once the worry is inside of the rock, if you live near water, go there and throw that rock in. If you don't live near the water, a little hole in the garden will do the trick. By the way, this also works for adults!

You might also want to visualize using rocks without the use of actual rocks. Close your eyes and visualize a beautiful blanket laying on the floor, with several little rocks on it. Name your worries, and as you do so, place each worry within a rock. When all of your worries are contained within the rocks and placed on the blanket, see the Worry Committee as they begin to arrive, pulling a large cart. The Worry Committee will be fun for you to create – each committee will be different. The Worry Committee will then gather all of the rocks and place them in the cart. You may wish to make a bit of a farewell speech to the worries and the Worry Committee as they move down the dusty trail. Be assured that those rocks will be going to The Worry Recycle Depot where they will be recycled into sand for a beautiful, far away beach, or perhaps made into magic fairy dust to be used in other visualizations.

The Scary Monster

My granddaughter, Madeline, has recently discovered scary monsters – not unusual for a three-year-old. When her mom tucked her into bed one night, Madeline began to talk about how afraid she was of the scary monsters. Her mom listened, empathized, and then asked Madeline what they looked like. Well, she's only just three, so they looked…scary. She was a little short on detail, but that's okay. Her mom explained to her that scary monsters are just little guys who actually want to find a friend, but they have really bad manners so they don't know how to be friends.

She then asked Madeline if she thought she could try to be a friend to the scary monsters, because that would make them feel really happy. Madeline answered in the affirmative, but apparently the look on her face said otherwise. Happily, Madeline came to the breakfast table the following morning, eager to talk about her new scary monster friends. She was able to visualize, at the age of three, an outcome that was not so scary.

I wonder if our anxiety is a little bit like a scary monster – aggressive and frightening, with really bad manners, rudely interrupting us at the most inopportune times. Perhaps if we befriend that scary monster, like Madeline did, it won't be so scary after all.

Loved Ones

One worry that many of us have, including Michelle at the outset of this book, is what might be happening to our loved ones when they are out of our sight. I cannot imagine the worry that many American people have every single day, given the out-of-control gun violence in their country, when their children go off to school. We worry about our little ones, and we continue to worry about them as they get older and begin to experience what the world has to offer. Will they play ball today or will they take opioids? Will they do homework or will they take the car for a drive and be in a terrible accident? We cannot be with them 24 hours a day. We simply cannot protect them from all imagined (or real) danger. We do not have that control.

For many of us, our worries are mostly unjustified; our children are safe. But what about the families who are not safe? What about the families whose children are taken from them forcibly and put in detention facilities, simply because they were fleeing even more dangerous circumstances in their home country? Can you imagine the trauma these children (and their parents) experience because of this separation? This uncertainty, this danger of separation, is sure to cause untold damage. Encouraging these parents to *become calm* is nothing short of ridiculous. They are without power and cannot affect a positive outcome. As human beings, must we not come together to make sure these children are safe and living with the parents who love them? Every day I am grateful that I live in Canada. I am very proud to be a Canadian citizen. I feel safe in my compassionate and generous country and hold my fellow Canadians in the highest regard.

Our minds can create all kinds of scenarios that are negative or perhaps even catastrophic, whether faced with real danger or no danger at all. When you think about what just happened as you read about the situations above, I'm quite sure that you'll realize how visualization played a part in any anxiety you might be feeling right now. I would like to urge you instead to use visualization to create calm within you, especially for those of you who are, in fact, not in imminent danger.

Let's think about it. You control your thoughts, feelings, and behavior, and how you respond to the world around you. This means that you do not control what happens to your mate and your children when they walk out the door. You do not control what happens to your friend, your lover, your sister, or brother. You do not have that power. You can love them and you can support them, but you can not control what happens in their lives. How might we use visualization to help you to remain calm?

When you begin to feel anxiety about your loved one, first think about what you control and what you do not control. I used to feel anxious about my daughter when she was a teenager. It wasn't until she travelled in Australia in her early twenties, alone for some of that time, that I had no choice but to come to grips with the fact that I could not control what was happening to her. I had to let go of the *notion* that I did have that control. The way I handled this was to visualize her every morning, waking up to a new day, and when I could see her clearly in my mind's eye, I would create beautiful golden rays of sunlight that would encircle her, keeping her safe. These rays of light were so strong that absolutely nothing could penetrate them. I would fill the rays with love and say, "Blessings on your day, daughter of mine." In doing this, I felt a measure of peace. Every time the anxiety tried to creep back in I would envision her again surrounded by this beautiful protective shield. This visualization got me through some difficult days.

Clara's Black Hole

I mentioned previously that being able to locate and describe where and how you feel anxiety in your body is the essential first step to using visualization to reduce that anxiety. You may recall how I would hang my Gone Fishing sign on my office door, creating the privacy I needed to lay down on the floor and visualize without interruption. Or you may recall the story of my grandson, his fear of thunder, and how we used the visualization of the fish in his tummy, depicting his fear and anxiety, and how his Fairy Godmother brought a magic blanket to lay over the fish to quiet them. Let's do one more example to help you further understand how this stuff works.

For purposes of anonymity, I am going to again amalgamate a couple of my clients into one, and we'll call her Clara. Clara was experiencing a high degree of anxiety, to the point where she was almost unable to leave her home. We talked about where in her body she felt that anxiety. It seemed to centre in her abdominal area, causing her to feel really sick to her stomach and very shaky. I asked Clara to close her eyes and visualize this anxiety. First, I asked her what it looked like. Clara described the anxiety as being just a big black hole. I actually hear this description quite often from clients – black, empty, nothing. Clara was adamant that there was nothing there. I wondered to myself how we could describe this nothing, and I decided to ask Clara, because she is obviously the expert in the area of her own anxiety.

Despite my inquiry, Clara maintained that there was nothing there. A big black hole. No smell. No shape. No activity. Nothing. I asked her to look deeper…and deeper still. Still nothing. Often when my client and I look deeper into the black hole, something materializes. Not this time. The course of action became apparent to me. I knew it was important to keep looking, because just as numbness can be painful, so too can nothingness be full of important things.

I suggested that we call upon her helper to work with us to finally *see* what that nothingness was all about. I always encourage my clients to choose the helper that appeals to them. For some, it is a Fairy Godmother or Wise Old Woman, a Super Hero, or perhaps a male Sage. For others, it may be a beloved ancestor, long gone. It might be a mythical creature, a Warrior Brave, a Shaman, or even a

Spirit Animal who comes to you. I was once visited by a Crocodile, and learned some important information from him!

I was also surprised to discover that in my own visualizations, both my Grandfathers came forward to help me. One of them died before I was born, and the other was 75 years old when I was born, and I didn't really know him very well. But there they were, front and centre in my visualizations, ready to help me. At other times, I have had a wise old woman, whom I affectionately named Lady Gillian. My point is this – our brain will conjure up a helper for us, if we want it to. It won't always be the same helper.

Back to Clara. Clara summoned her grandmother, who had always been, until her death, a solid figure in Clara's life. Her grandmother represented stability and unconditional love to her. Grandmother arrived, and I suggested to Clara that she ask her grandmother to help her find something in the darkness. Sure enough, after some looking, grandmother found a tiny spark of light, right in the centre of the darkness. I suggested that we ask grandmother to grow the light bigger and bigger, to shed a little light, so to speak, on the anxiety. What we found, as the light grew brighter, were sharp, angular hook-like objects, black, digging into her centre. We went through the steps.

- What do they look like? What color are they? What shape are they? Large or small? Close together or far apart?
- If you touch them, are they smooth or rough? Wet or dry? Slippery or not?
- Do they have a smell? What is that smell?
- What kind of activity are they doing? Are they still or moving? Are they digging in or flying around?

What Clara described was this. The black hooks were L shaped, with the hook on the end of the L. They were neither large nor small but were all the same size. They would fly around, careening off of one another until the hook would dig into her centre, and become lodged, growing roots deep into her body. Clara wanted them gone.

I suggested to Clara that she ask grandmother to help, and that she let grandmother choose how she would do that. Sure enough, as I led Clara through the visualization, grandmother had a solution. Grandmother happened to have some healing light that was dispensed by a laser beam. One zap of the laser beam was able to still the frantic movement of the hooked objects, and with careful aim and precision, this same laser beam was able to target the roots and disintegrate them. Three cheers for grandmother!

I don't like to leave any empty spaces after a visualization. I want to ensure that there is no place for the anxiety to creep back in. Clara and I were able to continue the visualization, and with grandmother's assistance, put a beautiful, protective cloak over her entire abdomen, a sort of shield to prevent more black hooks from taking up residence. Again, we visualized that cloak in great detail. Once the cloak was in place, I asked Clara how she was feeling, and she was feeling as I expected – calm, peaceful, and still. I let Clara know that any time she experienced that anxious feeling in her abdomen again, she would be able to call upon her grandmother for help. The visualization is hers, and can always be a powerful tool for her to help her tame her anxiety.

I urge you to make visualization an important part of your anxiety-taming plan. The results will be powerful, effective, and most likely immediate. If it doesn't work for you right away, keep working at it. It will become easier and more effective each time you try.

CHAPTER TWENTY-THREE
Balanced Self Care

Seriously, balanced self-care is essential to our well-being. It took me 50 years to learn this, and once I was able to figure it out, I was significantly more content and more at peace with myself. When I stopped drinking alcohol and basically did an overhaul of my life, I began to think about the importance of all the parts of me – the mental, the physical, the emotional, and the spiritual. I knew that learning (the mental part of me) was essential to my feeling of joy and fulfillment. I decided to return to university to complete a Master's Degree. Physically, I overhauled my home – got rid of all the junk food and the alcohol, and fired up the treadmill. Emotionally, I reached for connection with sober people, and limited my contact with people who drank alcohol regularly. With respect to the spiritual, I began to consider in earnest what *spiritual* actually meant for me. This is how I began to construct balanced self care – small but steady steps. Movement creates movement!

First, I want to address the issue of self-care vs. self*ish*. More often than not, when broaching the notion of self-care with my clients, many of them feel guilty even *thinking* about self care, never mind doing something about it. It feels very selfish to think about setting aside time for themselves, especially if they are women.

Frequently, when I ask women to place themselves on the ladder of self-care, I get the same sorry answer, in words similar to this:

"I'm not even on the ladder. I'm lying on the floor beside the ladder."
Who do you think might be on the ladder? Husband, children, job,
parents, church, volunteer work, etc. The order varies, but while
others have a place on the ladder, the women often feel they do not.

Balanced self-care, as I said, incorporates mental, physical, emotional, and spiritual well-being – each one an important aspect of caring for one's self. During different phases of my life, I have been good at taking care of the different aspects of self-care, at different times, but never able to take care of all four at the same time. One of my biggest hurdles that I have needed to overcome, time and again, is the amount of time I have dedicated to work versus the amount of time I have dedicated to self-care. I talked about self-care all the time with my clients, and yet, I struggled with my own.

It was not until my body talked to me, with a serious spike in blood pressure, that I realized that what I was doing was, in all likelihood, going to shorten my life. I was still learning, in my 60s. I was self-employed, working about 10 hours a day, counselling people, doing reports, doing my own bookkeeping, and generally having no time for much else. When the work day ended, I felt much too tired to go out for a walk, get to a class, or anything else. I was working hard and busy enough that I was turning clients away, something I really hated to do. But it was not until my body gave me a wake-up call that I realized something had to change.

It was at this point that I decided to treat myself as if I were a client. I made sure that every single day I incorporated time for me to care for myself mentally, physically, emotionally, and spiritually, going so far as to pencil myself into my own daily appointment calendar. It seemed at the time that this was the only way I could make it happen.

My work day was quickly shortened to seven hours a day (all I had to do was say no). This left me the time, and more importantly for me, the energy, for walks, yoga, visiting friends, reading, learning new things, connecting with family, and so on. I was much happier when I did this.

261

Now I am semi-retired, feeling in a good place mentally, emotionally, and spiritually. I continue to work on my physical goals, and I'm feeling good about that too. Sometimes I don't want to stop writing to go to the gym, but I've discovered that my brain works better after a break, especially if that break incorporates some physical activity.

Self-Care Assessment and Goals

Self-care is about the responsibility we each have of meeting our own needs. It cannot be done *to* us or *for* us. You may discover that you need to negotiate with your partner or your children to get the time that you require for self-care. Explain to them how you will be more present to them if you are cared for and healthy yourself. How do we go about creating our own self-care plan?

Let's take a first step. Find a decent sized piece of paper, draw a circle, and divide it into four quadrants. At the top, write *My Balanced Self-Care.* On the outside of each quadrant, label the quadrants *Physical, Mental, Emotional,* and *Spiritual.*

To begin this exercise, I want you to write down what you are already doing each week to care for yourself mentally, physically, emotionally, and spiritually (guidelines below). Once you have completed that aspect, I would like you to consider adding one or two things to each category, depending on how full your schedule is. Conversely, if you find that your schedule is full to the point of overflowing, consider what you might be able to remove. An important aspect of self-care is time to do... nothing at all. But here is the important part of this exercise – all four of the quadrants must be balanced. It is not healthy to have your mental quadrant full to overflowing and your physical quadrant empty. Below are some ideas for how to look at each category. I'm sure you'll have many more ideas of your own.

Physical Self-Care

- Exercise: Walk, swim, run, dance, garden, hike, work out at the gym, yoga, jazzercize, Zumba, climb a tree, do team sports – virtually anything you can dream up that is safe and gets you moving!

- Nutrition: Healthy foods, regular meals, less sugar and fewer carbs, and a variety of food.

- Financial Security: Are you living within your means? Do you have a budget? Are financial issues causing you stress? Would you benefit from professional help? Whatever it might be, tend to it.

- Medical: Attend to illness, body parts needing care, take prescribed medications appropriately, moderate or stop consumption of alcohol, practice recreational drug safety, (I encourage abstinence, or at least serious moderation, for so many reasons!) dental cleaning and checkups, eye examinations, and an annual checkup with your family doctor.

- Body care: Clean body, clean clothes, brush your teeth, comb your hair, clean your fingernails. Options: hair cuts, manicure or pedicure, massage, or any other treatment that you can afford that feels good for you.

- Enough (but not too much) rest and sleep. Target seven to eight hours a night.

Mental Self-Care

- Consider how you use your brain, how you express your creativity, and what you love to learn.

- Learn something new at home and at work. Take a class, read, study, or follow a pattern to create or build something new. Forget the pattern – dream up your own creation.

- Do something creative – sew, garden, build something, paint, draw, sing, write songs, play an instrument, dance, quilt, write in a journal, take photographs, color, invent something – what do you love to do that puts you *in the zone*?

- Do crossword puzzles, brain teasers, jigsaw puzzles – anything that stretches your brain in a new direction.
- Join a discussion group or planning committee. Volunteer to be a director on a board.

Emotional Self-Care

- Connect with a friend or family member you can share with.
- Give emotional support to others, perhaps family, friends, fellow co-workers. Accept emotional support from others. If you don't have that support, find it.
- Become aware of people who are leaching from your pool of emotional well-being. If you find that someone is coming to you over and over again with the same negative complaints, get them to stop by simply saying, "What do you think you can do about that?" Repeat those words as often as necessary. You can also remind them that you are solution focused, interested in hearing the problem only once, and then from that time forward you want only to discuss potential solutions with them.
- Talk with your doctor if you're experiencing distress because of grief or mental health concerns. Your doctor will help you to find the appropriate help.
- Talk with a therapist.
- Join a support group.
- Be a volunteer – you will receive much more than you give!
- Take time to be alone, to have quiet time.
- Do some journaling.
- Listen to your body – it will sometimes alert you to emotions you don't know you're feeling.

- Work hard to think positively; no what-iffing.
- Decide to stop being an anxious person; learn the strategies to lessen your anxiety.

Spiritual Self-Care

- Keep in mind that spiritual means different things to different people. Focus on what it means to you.
- Connect with nature, with animals.
- Connect with other humans, socially or through volunteer work.
- If you are religious, attend church, mosque, or temple, and participate in groups where you see a good fit for yourself.
- Pray.
- Meditate.
- Be still. Indulge in silence.
- Consider meaning and purpose in your life – do you want or need to make changes?
- Connect spiritually through art and music.
- Give back to others in your community. You will find that as you focus on the needs of others, your focus on your own anxiety will diminish.

Now you have the idea. Once you have a few things happening in each category, you will find that your life nicely balances itself, creating more peace and contentment. As you are feeling more balanced, more peaceful, and more content, your anxiety levels will decrease.

Self-care is something I review often, to ensure that I am still in balance. There will be times when you are doing more of one, and less of another, but overall, it is optimal if they can generally be balanced.

CHAPTER TWENTY-FOUR
Odds and Sods

I'm thinking about my choice of title for this bit. Thinking about the word "sods." It means what you would expect – tufts of grass, pieces of lawn, or pieces of earth. I guess the *odds* part of the title is about the strategies I want to share with you that didn't fit anywhere else. The sods part? Well, it's all about taking root and growing, isn't it? That's what I hope all the strategies you've learned will do – take root and grow. I hope that you will *use* some of the strategies that I've shared with you, and I also hope that you will be motivated to create your own. (Get out your highlighter and put the focus on the strategies that appeal to you.) Above all, I hope that you will share your strategies with others who have anxiety.

Here are my odds and sods:

- Selfie Hug: at least, this is what it feels like to me. Place one hand on your heart, and one hand over your belly button. Apply gentle pressure. Breathe. It makes no difference which hand rests on which body part – do whatever is most comfortable for you. Remain in this position, breathing in and out, until your body feels calmer. I don't know why this works, but it works for me and for many of the people I have shared it with.

- Stimulate your brain: For ten to twenty minutes a day, focus on a crossword puzzle, brain games, learning a short poem or creating your own, do math puzzles – whatever interests you. It will help your brain to refocus on something other than your anxiety.

- Remember that there's a fine line between anxiety and excitement. Sometimes when I think I am feeling anxious, what I am actually feeling is excitement. One is positive, one is not. I recall a man who had decided to make a change in his life and he was excited about making it. But when the change was imminent, he began to feel anxious. He'd perhaps forgotten that this change was something that he'd chosen for himself, and that it was positive.

- Don't be afraid to admit when you don't know something or you don't understand something. Genetics is a very complex field of study, and when I was writing the two or three paragraphs about RNA and DNA, I began to feel anxious, because this science is difficult for me to understand, and my knowledge and experience are seriously limited. I did a reality check. I realized that anyone reading this book will not expect me to be an expert in genetics, but that they may appreciate my efforts to provide a simplified explanation. I am a clinical therapist, not a geneticist, and my goal is to share strategies that will help you with your anxiety. By doing this reality check, I was able to let go of my anxiety.

- Ensure that your work-life balance *is in balance.* Seriously!

- Avoid the trap of seeing everything in black and white. Nothing is all bad, but if it does feel all bad at that moment, remember – it won't remain that way forever. Change happens in our lives continuously, more quickly when we are open to it.

- Recognize opportunities. To do that, you will need to stop listening to your own anxious self-talk. Anxiety takes up a lot of your amazing brain function. It's time to clear some space.

- When you're unsure about the next step, wait. Believe that if you wait, the right thing will happen.

- Try something new – new food, new recipe, new music, new exercise, new class, new neighborhood for a walk – this will help to take your mind off your own anxiety.

- Make a conscious choice to be content. I personally think that the word *happy* is highly over-rated and can create ridiculous expectations. There is no such thing as being happy all the time. As a rebel in my 20's, I thought that if you were content, you would be doomed to a life of mediocrity. *Nothing* could be worse, right? Wrong. How very naïve I was. Now I believe that contentment is more precious than happiness. I urge you to always look for things in your environment, big or small, that promote that feeling of contentment in you. Express your gratitudes when you find them. As I'm writing this, I realize that I feel great joy about the just-right coffee cup that I'm holding in my hand. This cup is the perfect size for me, textured to the touch, nicely rounded, with hand-painted blue hearts on it. It even has dainty little feet at the base. It's my *special moment* cup and it makes me feel ridiculously content.

- Express your sense of humour – yes, we all have one! Laugh at yourself. Try a yoga laughter class – it's a riot!

Using humour to combat your own anxiety will also decrease the anxiety of the people around you. I recall a client I worked with (we'll call him John) who had such intense anxiety that he spent all his energy trying to control his own environment, to the point that his children were really suffering. He was devastated by the pain that he was causing them. He ran a 'tight ship,' demanding that his children have impeccable manners and behaviour. John asked me what he could do about that. We brain-stormed a few possibilities, and our next session was filled with laughter as he told me how his plan unfolded. What was especially delightful about this plan was that it was all his own creation.

John prepared a big feast of chicken and dumplings, and when he sat down with his children to eat, he gave them his usual stern look. They all ate silently, until he stood up and ceremoniously turned his plate of food upside-down on the table. His children gasped, fearing the worst. He burst out laughing. He told me that, one by one, his children also started to laugh, and from that day forward, their home was, for the most part, a much happier place. Hearing about that mess and that laughter reinforced for me that we can change our reality, and we can impact the lives of our loved ones in a positive way by doing so. Sometimes, to make things right, we simply have to turn them upside down.

- Get outside of yourself and your anxious world. Do some volunteer work. Knowing that you are contributing to another's well-being will lessen your focus on yourself and your anxiety and very possibly create a sense of well-being within you too.

- Overthinking? Instead of becoming anxious about the fact that you are overthinking, befriend and welcome your Overthinker by naming it – perhaps its name is Calamitous Cathy, Repeating Ronnie, Grinding Gilda, or Stuck Stevie. Let your Overthinker know that you see her, you HEAR her, and enough is enough. Give your Overthinker a friendly bon voyage and refocus on something that is worthy of your time and energy. Perhaps your Overthinker can just get on the bus!

- Combat boredom. Boredom can lead to rumination which can lead to anxiety. Too much time on your hands can lead to what-iffing!

- Play with children. Nothing grounds me as soundly as playing with my grandchildren, listening to their voices, creating stories with them, laughing with them, seeing the joy and wonder in their eyes, and holding them close – they are a miracle of delight.

- I have talked about the importance of breathing, but I'll repeat it here. Five deep breaths in (thinking *slow* on the in breath) and five deep breaths out (thinking *down* on the out breath). Do this several times a day to maintain a calm body, and a clear mind.

- Watch your internal monologue. Eliminate stress/ anxiety words.

- If multi-tasking makes you anxious, stop doing it. Do one thing at a time. Set *reasonable* goals for your day.

- Manage distractions. Don't stop what you're doing to do something else that has popped into your head. Put it on your list to do later.

- Don't fix something that is not broken. Especially do not try to fix something if it's not yours to fix.

- Consider yoga. It is always my best stress reliever. It has also helped me to connect to my body – essential for locating and visualizing anxiety in my body. If not yoga, any kind of exercise, anything at all that gets you moving. I haven't spent much time on this, because the jury is no longer out. The verdict is clear – exercise makes a huge difference in terms of decreasing and managing both anxiety and depression. Just do it!

- Listen to tranquil music. Or dance up a storm.

- Do housework (sure works for me).

- Get a pet. Loving and stroking a pet is an excellent way to calm your body.

- Progressive muscle relaxation. Start with your toes, work your way up your body; tighten each muscle group, and then *flop* the muscles to allow them to totally relax. Finish with your face. After tightening all the muscles, completely relax your face and let your mouth hang open, take a nice deep breath, and enjoy that drooly feeling.

- Social connection. Join a support group, start a monthly dinner club with friends, do volunteer work, play cards, join a curling team, take dance lessons, attend a football game, or join a book club. Social connection will take you out of yourself and create the sense of well being that comes from connection with others. If you are an introvert, remember to connect in a way that is comfortable for you.

- Drop burdens that aren't yours. You can't carry everyone's burdens. They are too heavy and you will fall over!

- When things seem *all bad*, find the one bright spot in your life and make it grow.

- Reduce alcohol and caffeine consumption. They both play havoc with your entire system and can set off anxiety. (Ever heard of drunkard's remorse? I think that's a combination of guilt and anxiety.)

- Be mindful that the THC in marijuana creates anxiety in some people. If you need medical marijuana, get a prescription and use the product that has much less THC.

- Meditation: find 10 to 20 minutes a day to meditate. This will help you to clear your head, focus, and fully relax mentally, physically, and emotionally.

- Dig in the dirt. This digging in dirt will provide you with the opportunity to get some exercise and fresh air. I read somewhere that research suggests that after thirty minutes of gardening, our stress hormones are lower. Studies have shown a link between a common bacterium found in garden soil and increased serotonin levels.

- Selfie Hug Number Two: wrap your arms right around yourself and give yourself a big hug. Even your own touch will release oxytocin and promote your sense of well being.

- Hug your family. I am so lucky that my daughter and my grandchildren are such good huggers. We never part from each other without a big hug.

- Be mindful of your diet. Junk food will make you feel like... well, junk. Healthy food – especially fruits, vegetables, seeds, nuts, and some grains (and meat for the meat lovers) will make you feel like an empowered human being. You get to choose – junked or empowered. Drink LOTS of water!

- Movement creates movement. Strive to walk ten thousand steps a day, especially if you're not otherwise active. If you have been very sedentary, check with your Doctor before starting a new exercise program. Try to do physical activities that are fun for you.

- Send loving messages to your body and your brain throughout the day. When is the last time you thanked your body for carrying you all these many years? When is the last time you sent some love to your brain to thank it for being so amazing and brilliant?

- Do anything – *anything* – creative! Cook, garden, paint, weld, sing, dance, draw, whittle, write, quilt, sew, build – *anything!*

- Finally, and most importantly, be your own best friend. Speak to yourself and treat yourself as you would your best friend. It's that simple.

IN CLOSING
Attitude of Gratitude

A few years ago, I listened to a television presentation about happiness, and how we might increase our happiness level. Keeping in mind that I am now more interested in contentment than happiness, I decided to do the daily practice that might increase my happiness quotient anyway, mostly out of curiosity. I was quite excited and asked a few people if they would do the project with me. None of them were interested in doing it with me, and one of them actually said, "I don't have time." I remember thinking "You don't have time to be happier?"

But that didn't stop me. I set out to complete the project, and I found that it really did make a measurable difference in my life. I continue the practice, which is basically one of being positive, grateful, active, spreading a little sunshine to other people, letting people know that I care about them, and telling them when they have had a positive impact on my life.

I began to record, every 24 hours, three things that I was grateful for. I decided that it had to be something within the last 24 hours, and it had to be specific. It didn't count if I said, "I'm grateful for my family." It was more likely to be something along the lines of, "I'm grateful for my daughter. She knew I was a little off today, and went out of her way to help me feel better, simply by asking and caring."

I quickly learned that becoming aware of what I am grateful for and stating it aloud or in writing is a very mindful experience. I became more mindful of the good things in my life, because I was always looking for something to be grateful about. After all, I needed something to write in my journal. It didn't take long before I started seeing more and more things that inspired me, or filled me with awe, or created joy and peace within me.

I recall early one morning, about 6 a.m., I was out for a walk. Suddenly, overhead, I saw the biggest flock of birds I had ever seen in my life. It was big enough that I was awed by it. There was a young man standing across the street from me, with his lunch bucket, waiting for the bus to take him to work. He looked up when I did, and then we looked at each other, sharing that special moment. It was really a moment of connection for me, first with the birds, and then with the young man.

I have had clients, especially my depressed or anxious clients, tell me that they were unable to find one single thing to be grateful for in a seven-day period. I explain to them that they don't need to find something huge. It is okay to be grateful for the peanut butter on their toast, or grateful that their big toe doesn't hurt, or grateful that they have tissue to blow their nose. The point is to get your brain looking in the direction of *positive*. Once you have it pointed in the right direction, with a little nudge here and there, you'll find that your brain will automatically want to find positive things that you are, indeed, grateful for.

Basically, if something makes you smile, or fills you with joy, or makes you want to dance, you can absolutely be grateful for it. Sometimes we can simply acknowledge that someone has given us help, or that a gadget has made our lives easier. Or perhaps we have learned something new, or found a new perspective, or an understanding with another person – we can be grateful for all of this. If something shows you that your world is precious, or that you are precious, that is something to be really grateful for.

As a part of my project, I purposely increased the number of smiles I was giving out in a day. Maybe these smiles went to my loved ones, or maybe to complete strangers. Smiling is the gift that keeps on giving.

The muscles we use to smile can be stimulated even when we don't feel like smiling. Try putting a pencil between your teeth. The muscles used for smiling will be stimulated, and your brain will get tricked into thinking you are actually smiling, activating the plea-sure response in your brain. The first several times that I tried it, I burst out laughing. Partly because I felt ridiculous, and maybe, just maybe, I was getting a little dopamine. Whatever the reason, it made me feel better.

I also made an effort to connect socially more often. I'm becoming more and more introverted as I age, content with my own company for the most part. But other times, I feel lonely and want meaning-ful connection. I find that I enjoy my solitude much more after I have been in the company of others. I have also found that I feel really good when I tell someone else what they mean to me and how they impact me positively. Part of the reason I feel so good is because I know I'm making someone else feel good. The other part to that is that I am sharing a part of myself, in a positive way. It's all about connection.

I can't stress this enough: feeling and expressing gratitude is the foundation to creating less anxiety in your life.

It's simple, really. Draw yourself a circle, and fill it up with little circles, making it completely full. Write the word anxiety in each little circle. Now... do you have room for anything other than anxiety in that big circle? No, I think not.

Now draw a second circle. Fill it up completely with little circles, and in half of them, write the word anxiety. For the other half, write the word gratitude. Hmmmm. Now you only have room for half the anxiety that you used to have.

You guessed it. Draw your last circle. Fill it up with little circles. In each circle, write the word gratitude. Do you have any room for anxiety? See what I mean?

Sometimes Things are Mighty Good

When I was six years old, I went to the local movie theatre with my older brother and sister, and we saw *Old Yeller*. My mom told me that this movie had quite an impact on me. Apparently, when I got home from the movie, I was crying with such intensity that I couldn't even tell her about the story. A few years ago, I found a line from the book *Old Yeller,* and it pretty much sums up how I hope you have come to think about anxiety, and the place it has in your life. It basically said that when difficult things happen in our lives, it feels very harsh and unfair, but that life also has some really good things in it too, and if we waste all of our time and energy worrying about the bad stuff, we will miss out on the good stuff, and then, well, everything just seems bad. There is a lot of truth to that.

I met a woman in the gym parking lot one day who really brought this home to me. I'd never spoken to her before, but I'd overheard conversations she'd had with others, and I found her comments to be mostly negative. It was a beautiful, sunny, clear, warm fall day in my part of Canada, and after we said good morning, she said, "It's too windy out today." I felt sad for her. There was, in fact, a very light breeze – something that softly kissed my face – nothing to be fussed about. But this woman was unable to focus on the stunning beauty of this fall day, because she was fully focused on the wind and how it was all wrong. I wondered how her life might be different if she could, every day, feel gratitude for the small things, and the joy that accompanies that precious feeling.

Writing this book has been a mighty good experience for me. I have shared what I know with the hope that what I've learned will help you to tame your anxiety and enable you to move forward boldly and sure-footedly. Now is the time for me to stop. Now is the time for you to take the opportunity to make changes in your thinking, choose your strategies, get your brain on straight, work your strategies, and enjoy the results.

I want you to know that as you move forward, there will be moments when you stumble, but that is really okay; we all stumble. We stumble and we get up; we stumble again, and we get up again. We are each a work in progress. Every time you lose your footing, you will get up stronger and surer than you were before; you will move forward more confidently into the life that you are meant to live. You can do this.

MY GRATITUDES

This book has been my labour of love, and I am grateful to so many people for their support and expertise along the way. There have been many teachers in my life, and I especially want to thank my family members, friends, and clients who have struggled with anxiety. Your experiences have informed my own, and I am truly grateful to each of you. I hope that I have, in some small measure, helped you to manage the beast.

My gratitude to anyone who has ever been my teacher in a class-room setting or work environment (and that includes drumming around the campfire!). You have positively contributed to my understanding of and passion about this thing we call anxiety.

To my guide, Friesen Press. Kim Schacht was friendly, patient, and professional, responding to all of my questions with enough detail and clarity to set my mind at ease. Although she was the first person I spoke with, I called her my "Closer" because she sealed the deal for me. Miko Heddle worked alongside me throughout the creation of this book. She was my go-to person, and this meant that she had to know pretty much everything, be well organized, and have great ideas, while calmly and creatively accomplishing some things that seemed insurmountable to me. She far exceeded my expectations in all of these roles, and I am deeply grateful to her for helping me to create the finished product.

To my Leon Elliot Nadin Barrett for painting (with a little bit of help from his mom) a beautiful butterfly to grace the cover of this book. You will always be my most special boy in the whole world!

Special gratitude to Tareina Hunt at Nut-Nae Art Websites & Graphics for seeing Leon's butterfly and knowing that it was *the one,* and then beautifully creating the front and back covers that please me so much, because they are exactly right. You understood my vision and brought it to life. Gratitude also for helping me with the world of websites and other technological matters. Your collaboration means more to me than I can express here. Readers: If you want someone who will take your passion, hold it with care, and then create your vision for all the world to see, you can find Tareina at www.nutnaeart.com.

Gratitude to Loraine Smith, my Forever Best Bastard. You know my heart and I know yours. I don't know why I get to have you in my life, but I am grateful every day that I do.

To the Tenold women, gratitude for being my other family, for my entire life. You anchor me.

Claudia Tenold, of Ten Old Books, for sharing your time, knowledge, and expertise, encouraging me from the very outset when everyone, including me, felt uncertain that this passion of mine would actually become a real book. Thank you for being the person who saw some promise in that first draft!

Humongous gratitude to my readers, Carrie Bahm, Aleitha Ward, Brenda Tenold, Norma Green, Judy Walker, Michele McCue and Glenda Hanson. You have all given generously of your time and experience, and I thank you for your great suggestions. Your wisdom has been my gift.

To my small but powerful group of Writing Women, thank you for showing me that less is more. I love the time we spend together.

To my Book Clubs (past and present), thank you for enjoying the written word with me. I'm always excited to see what discussion the next book will bring.

To H.H. – you showed me that it can be done. I am so proud of you!

Gratitude to Michelle Magafas Flood, Theresa Lutz, Heather Knoblock Cottrell, and Judy Walker. You enrich our lives by courageously sharing your struggles and your strategies with us.

Gratitude for my family, Terry and Leone Marcotte, Beverly and Brian Harding, Sharon Marcotte, and Deborah Marcotte. Even though we're spread out across Canada and sometimes the United States, I know that you are only a phone call away, and I am grateful that I was born into a family such as ours.

Gratitude for my parents Ernest Marcotte and Doreen Johnson Marcotte. Even though they are no longer with me on this earth, they are always with me. I am so grateful for their wisdom and love, and for encouraging me to be all that I can be – always with the expectation that if I did my best, that would be exactly right, and it would be enough.

For one of the most important people in my life, my grandmother, Gudrun Ryan Johnson. Grandma taught me how to laugh at myself, how to love the power of connection, and how to feel and express compassion and kindness. Grandma was my first hero. Good night, good night, Grandma.

To my beautiful grandchildren, Leon Elliot and Madeline Harper – you fill me up with joy, laughter, and love. Thank you for letting me tell stories about you. You constantly amaze me with your wisdom and your generosity of spirit.

To Russell Nadin – you are the absolute best son-in-law a mother could ever hope for. I love that my daughter had the wisdom to pick you, and that you had the wisdom to pick her right back.

Jennifer Barrett, daughter of mine, you have accompanied me on this journey every step of the way, caring about this work, sharing your love, encouragement, and expertise as an editor. I literally could not have done this without you, and I am forever grateful for you! Any errors found are mine and mine alone. How lucky I am that you chose me to be your mother. Move over Gudrun – there's another hero in the family.

FURTHER READING
Some of the Books I Love

Ardagh, A. (2008) *Leap before you look: 72 shortcuts for getting out of your mind and into the moment.* Boulder: Sounds True, Inc.

Beattie, M. (2009) *The new codependency: help and guidance for todays' generation.* New York: Simon & Schuster

Cain, S. (2012) *Quiet: the power of introverts in a world that can't stop talking.* New York: Crown Publishers

Callahan, R. with Trubo, R. (2001) *Tapping the healer within.* New York: McGraw-Hill

Chopra, D. (1993) *Ageless body, timeless mind.* New York: Harmony Books

Cohen, G. (2005) *The mature mind: the positive power of the aging brain.* New York: Basic Books

Cornell, A. (1996) *The power of focusing: a practical guide to emotional self-healing.* Oakland: New Harbinger Publications

Curren, E. (2001) *Guided imagery for healing children and teens.* Hillsborough: Beyond Words Publishing, Inc.

Dallaire, R. with Beardsley, B. (2003) *Shake hands with the devil.* Toronto: Vintage Canada

Doidge, N. (2007) *The brain that changes itself.* New York: Penguin Group

Dorion, L.M. (2011) *Relatives with roots: a story about Metis women's connection to the land.* Saskatoon: Gabriel Dumont Institute

Hanh, T.N. (2010) *A pebble for your pocket: mindful stories for children and grown-ups.* Berkeley: Plum Blossom Books

Hanh, T.N. (2008) *Mindful movements: ten exercises for well-being.* Berkeley: Parallax Press

Harris, D. (2017) *Meditation for fidgety skeptics.* New York: Spiegel & Grau

Kingma, D. (2012) *When you think you're not enough: the four life-changing steps to loving yourself.* San Francisco: Conari Press

Maté, G. (2004) *When the body says no: the hidden cost of stress.* Toronto: Vintage Canada

MacLean, K. (2004) *Peaceful piggy meditation.* Park Ridge: Albert Whitman Prairie Paperback

Mlodinow, L. (2012) *Subliminal: how your unconscious mind rules your behavior.* New York: Pantheon Books

Plattor, C. (2010) *Loving an addict, loving yourself: the top ten survival tips for loving someone with an addiction.* Vancouver: Candace Plattor

Ratey, J. & Hagerman, E. (2008) *Spark: the revolutionary new science of exercise and the brain.* New York: Little, Brown and Company

Sams, J. (1994) *Earth medicine: the ancestors' ways of harmony for many moons.* San Francisco: Harper San Francisco

Schulz, M.L. (1998) *Awakening intuition.* New York: Three
Rivers Press

Simington, J. (2002) *Journey to the sacred: mending the fractured
soul.* Regina: Centax Books

Simington, J. (2010) *Setting the captive free.* Edmonton: Priority
Printing Ltd.

Smith, R. (1998) *Lessons from the dying.* Boston:
Wisdom Publications

Weiner-Davis, M. (1996) *Change your life and everyone in it.* New
York: Simon & Schuster Paperbacks

Williams, F. (2016) *My mind book.* USA: Fearless Assisted
Publishing Program

Documentary

Argot Pictures: POV series. *Almost sunrise.* PBS Television

Internet Links

https://www.sciencedaily.com/releases/2017/06/170615213301.
htm

http://www.cbc.ca/natureofthings/episodes/ptsd-beyond-trauma

https://www.facebook.com/Goals-Gratitude-223583261407464/

https://www.theglobeandmail.com/new/british-columbia/MDMA-
Assisted-Psychotherapy

http://lifeapprentice.net

http://www.nutnaeart.com

AnxietyChaosCalmed.com

Printed in Canada